Bitches in Bonnets

Life Lessons *from* Jane Austen's Mean Girls

SARAH J. MAKOWSKI

Prometheus Books

Guilford, Connecticut

⑱ Prometheus Books

An imprint of Globe Pequot, the trade division of
The Rowman & Littlefield Publishing Group, Inc.
4501 Forbes Blvd., Ste. 200
Lanham, MD 20706
www.rowman.com

Distributed by NATIONAL BOOK NETWORK

British Library Cataloguing in Publication Information Available

Library of Congress Cataloging-in-Publication Data

Names: Makowski, Sarah J., 1971– author.
Title: Bitches in bonnets : life lessons from Jane Austen's mean girls /
    Sarah J. Makowski.
Description: Lanham, MD : Rowman & Littlefield, [2023] | Includes
    bibliographical references. | Summary: "Bitches in Bonnets examines how six
    novels of quiet English life, penned by parochial Regency spinster Jane Austen,
    still provide insight on female relationships after all these years and how Austen's
    writing—and our reading of it—offers solace to millions of fans worldwide"
    —Provided by publisher.
Identifiers: LCCN 2022025367 (print) | LCCN 2022025368 (ebook) |
    ISBN 9781633888548 (paperback) | ISBN 9781633888555 (epub)
Subjects: LCSH: Austen, Jane, 1775–1817—Characters. | Austen, Jane, 1775–
    1817—Criticism and interpretation. | Women in literature. | Conduct of life in
    literature. | LCGFT: Literary criticism.
Classification: LCC PR4038.W6 M35 2023 (print) | LCC PR4038.W6 (ebook) |
    DDC 823/.7—dc23/eng/20220926
LC record available at https://lccn.loc.gov/2022025367
LC ebook record available at https://lccn.loc.gov/2022025368

To the fetch Janeites of the world.

Contents

Preface

It's actually Jane Austen who pushes
Louisa Musgrove off the slippery rocks.
—DIANE JOHNSON

Western women are in crisis. Not because of anything we did, but all the things we have to do. Even before COVID-19's disaster cocktail of working in improvised home offices while homeschooling, we've always been hustling. We juggle vast numbers of emotional and financial commitments, each vying for our full attention. Throw in an economic crisis, never-ending student debt, and misogynist politics, and it's no wonder that we're exhausted. At times like these, I turn to books. My immediate instinct in times of change is to hole up with cherished authors. They have been my best friends, my counselors when the world seems unglued. Fact or fiction, their teachings make almost anything seem manageable. I'm the target market for books on having a baby, buying a house, changing bad habits, and folding my clothes into tidy little packets that spark joy.

I read to relax and to escape, and if I'm lucky, to experience a happy ending through absolutely no effort of my own. Although I've lived in a non-English-speaking country for half of my life, I only read novels in my native language. Cuddling into bed with a great book whose every word I intuitively understand is comfort. No matter how good my German gets, reading it still feels like work. It probably isn't a surprise that Jane Austen and her safe world of family life and love are balsam to my soul.

After my father's sudden passing a few years ago, I took refuge the best way I knew how: with *Pride and Prejudice*. I have no idea how many times I've read it. Although I know exactly what each character will say and do, cheering and jeering them soothes almost any heartache I have ever had.

Dad's death happened at a very confusing time in my career. I had taken on a new role in a team of talented, bright women who just didn't seem to get along. Raised to be a pleaser, I struggled to deal with the disparate factions. On one side were a handful of women who wanted to advance quickly up the hierarchy. On the other were women happy to do the jobs they already had very well. Both groups were led by a perfectly lovely, perfectly mediocre, middle-aged white guy.

My euphoria at landing the role quickly dissolved. After just a few weeks, I began to feel like the nerdy band kid I was back in high school. The "cool girls," free from school runs, meal prep, and leaning in, were ready for unpaid overtime at the drop of a hat. They weren't interested in my best-practice bleating. Without knowing it, I had somehow morphed from an attractive, dedicated colleague to a grumpy, old curmudgeon who didn't put in enough effort.

"Effort," I abruptly learned, meant around-the-clock availability and an online presence that most working mothers of school-age kids simply can't afford.

This new landscape was perplexing. As an introvert with no sisters, I didn't have much experience with healthy female relationships growing up. My mom wasn't much help. Her answer to any spat I had with another girl at school was jealousy. In her world, women were judges. Whether fighting about looks, figures, clothes, or catching and keeping men, Mom taught me that other women should not be trusted.

Of course, after over two decades in the business world, I know that this simply isn't true. Most of my female colleagues and managers have been fantastic. Yet, a handful have bristled at collaborating closely with other women. This has always struck me as odd. Aren't we all in this together? Have I missed something important? Aren't we all underpaid and underrepresented? Haven't our foremothers fought to achieve great things for us, from universal suffrage to equal rights legislation? Aren't we all stretched too thin?

So why the (not-so-subtle) sabotage?

Researching this book, every woman I spoke to has had their own story to share. It starts on the playground, picking sides and whom to invite to birthday parties. Fueled by growing pains and raging hormones, it escalates in the drama that is high school. It follows us into adulthood when we're all struggling to define ourselves. New mothers aren't safe; the so-called Mommy Wars pit breastfeeders against bottle-feeders and Ferberizers against co-sleepers. Just yesterday, I learned that elementary school moms face public shaming by Instagram's female "lunchbox police."

Why do we make things harder for each other? As I settled in with Austen that terrible funeral weekend, I was ready to question just about everything. Reading about Elizabeth Bennet getting scorned yet again, I began to see parallels between Austen's fictional world and my own. Surely, I wasn't the first woman to be reminded of schoolyard cliques by snooty Caroline Bingley. Did other women recognize Lady Catherine de Bourgh's Karen-esque behavior from their own lives?

I knew that reading Austen couldn't change my father's passing. What she did offer was an insight into women misbehaving and a fresh perspective on my professional muddle. This book results from those initial questions and the wisdom of many women I have met along the way.

Jane Austen, it seems, already knew us—her modern readers.

On the surface, this seems implausible; marriage, the mission of all Austen's heroines, no longer carries the same economic and moral significance that it did in the nineteenth century. Contemporary Western women have career opportunities Georgian women likely never imagined. Women can earn, inherit, and retain their wealth as they see fit. Primogeniture is no longer the norm; in 2023, Princess Charlotte is lawfully ahead of her youngest brother in the line of succession to the British throne. For the most part, women can plan motherhood without a relationship with a man. Nevertheless, despite the appearance of radical change, Austen's characterizations of female experience capture human behaviors that continue to resonate.

This book is about the women in Austen's work, exploring how and why we still identify with the issues and behaviors she depicted two centuries ago. Although I use the binary applied during Austen's lifetime, I don't want to disrespect Austen's male, trans, or queer readership. The terminology is intended to keep the focus narrow for clarity and reflect my personal relationship with the content. I will leave the definition of female to the reader who identifies herself as female.

Of course, I know that many feminist men join me in adoring Austen. My teenage son counts on his ability to "speak Darcy" to get a girlfriend in college. Biographer Elizabeth Jenkins has even said that Austen "has probably given pleasure to more men in bed than any woman in history, except perhaps Agatha Christie." Nevertheless, I will persist with my gynocentric approach.

I doubt Austen would have minded. While she never got married, she did attract men's attention during her lifetime. The bloated and amoral Prince Regent, George IV, was an early collector of her novels. Prinny's librarian personally requested that Austen honor the monarch's admiration by writing a "Historical Romance illustrative of the august house of Cobourg." Austen bravely declined. In her refusal, she made her case quite clear, emphasizing her position as a female writer, unable (or unwilling) to write from any perspective but her own. She cautiously stated her inability to create "a Man's Conversation." Not even to save her own life, she claimed, could she bring such a story to life. Her sole compromise? A carefully worded, deceptively flowery-yet-somehow-snarky dedication to the acting monarch in her fourth published novel, *Emma*.

To this day, reports on Austen-related events inevitably depict male participants as anomalies. Journalist Sarah Lyall describes an Austen tour to the UK as "a group of highly literate ladies (and one gentleman)." Authors Ted Scheinman and William Deresiewicz cash in on this assumption with memoirs outlining their "accidental" Austen educations, their stories pivoting on the unlikeliness of their fandom. The same is true in TV and film. The Sheldon Coopers, Griggs, and

Joe Foxes of the world must be led to Austen by sensible women before they can appreciate her art.

The popular media image of the Janeite, or devoted Austen fan, is decidedly female. Extreme cases are pictured as bonnet-wearing fanatics like the heroine of the comic-novel-turned-film *Austenland*. Media reporting on Bath's annual Jane Austen Festival and the Jane Austen Society of North America's Annual General Meeting shows Janeites parading through streets or conference centers in Empire-waist dresses and attending frothy-sounding sessions on dance steps or Regency desserts. Despite their apparent frivolity, none of these events takes away from Austen's hypercanonical status or her fans' zeal.

Observing Austen's modern admirers is almost as fascinating as reading the novels themselves. Worship of "the divine Jane" is an event, a narrative worth reading not only by scholars but by us amateurs, as well. Her popularity has inspired countless studies, biblio-memoirs, and bibliotherapy accounts in recent decades. Some explore the history of Austen's fame and its cultural influence. Others look at how devotion to Austen has changed over time, continuing to evolve according to current social needs.

Among the books focused on Austen herself, the theme of looking for the "true" or "real" writer features heavily. With such little material to work with, scholars have had to dig deep, examining the few small, personal objects she left behind, as well as private memoirs and diaries of her family and acquaintances.

Social media has made life much easier for casual Janeites, who gather and commune on Facebook and Co. Austen lives on in an ever-expanding list of wonderfully named groups, from *Jane Austen Runs My Life*, to *Jane Austen Is Totally My Religion*, to *Jane Austen Is My Spirit Animal*. Fierce debates break out every day on the value of Austen films versus prose, or the (obvious superiority of the) 1995 *Pride and Prejudice* BBC miniseries versus the 2005 Hollywood adaptation (Team Firth!). Polls ask readers to name their favorite heroine, hero, protagonist, antagonist, and propose new actors for subsequent film versions. Selfies show modern Janeites on pilgrimage to Austen-related sites, joyfully collecting multiple editions of her novels, or holding puppies named Bingley.

The mainstream media inevitably portrays Janeites as white women. This image is slowly changing with the television production of Austen's novel fragment *Sanditon*, featuring a Black character from Austen's pen. The colorblind casting of Austen-adjacent projects like *Bridgerton* demonstrates that Regency fiction appeals to women of all colors. Blogs from a "sista's perspective" like *Black Girl Loves Jane* and the *Reclaiming Jane* podcast for "fans on the margins" indicate that the cliché of the lily-white, heteronormative Janeite is on its way out.

Austen isn't just a Western phenomenon. Janeites in Japan established a society in her honor in 2006, publishing manga versions of *Pride and Prejudice*, *Emma*, and *Sense and Sensibility*. *Pride and Prejudice* has been adapted in a justice system setting for South Korean television. Jane Austen Societies exist in India and Pakistan, with Austen's novels inspiring Bollywood and Tamil films and soap operas reflecting local marriage markets. According to *The Economist*, Austen is beloved in China for reflecting its traditional cultural values.

Adoration of "all things Jane" leads to thousands of Austen-inspired novels. Each month brings up to seventy new examples of Jane Austen Fan Fiction (JAFF) with scintillating titles such as *Pride and Prejudice and Zombies*, *Confessions of a Jane Austen Addict*, and *Mr. Darcy Broke My Heart*. Outside of the JAFF scene, contemporary bestselling authors depict their characters engaging with Austen's work. J. K. Rowling uses Austen characters as namesakes for her own. Both appropriations function as shorthand understood immediately by those in the know. Could a cat named Mrs. Norris be loveable?

With all this, is there anything left to be said about the author?

Virginia Woolf famously warned those brave enough to write about Austen, cautioning that "of all the great writers, she is the most difficult to catch in the act of greatness." That hasn't stopped many from attempting it. As novelist Douglas Glover elegantly observes, "academia has sacrificed entire forests to the altar of Jane Austen."

It's time to add my twig.

It may seem delusional, but I've attempted it nonetheless. Much has been written about Austen; I propose learning *through* her. Examining her wonderfully realistic, fault-prone female characters has taught me much about myself and others. Her work resonates with me—and millions like me—because her stories are also our stories.

My bitchy colleagues? Austen knew them.

Power struggles between adult women? Austen knew them.

Bad behavior among girls afraid for their futures? Austen knew it.

Since the dawn of civilization, these relationships have existed and are unlikely to die out anytime soon. Austen helps us look behind the curtain of animosity, hinting at its source. Inevitably, female aggression is born out of a sense of scarcity, whether time, money, resources, or love. The objects and efforts may *look* very different in the twenty-first century than in Austen's day, but the resulting behaviors and sting remain the same.

Then, as now, life can be overwhelming. We all have to maneuver between the needs of our families, workplaces, society, and often very last—ourselves. For me, Austen is at her best, her most rewarding, and most comforting, at the intersections between her fiction and my reality.

Literary professor Elaine Auyoung tells me that it doesn't matter how a fictional character resembles real life; after all, few of us are wandering the streets in bonnets these days. Instead, Auyoung explains, realism comes from "a reader's ability to construct, retrieve, and run mental models with ease." Austen's spare writing and broad descriptions make this easy for me and millions of others.

This book is for the fantastic, fetch Janeites who feel the same way. Whether we meet in person at conferences or on social media, these women tell me that yes, they know a Mrs. Elton, passive-aggressively judging Emma's wedding gown. Their daughters know high school Queen Bees like Isabella Thorpe, who control a highly codified popularity hierarchy. The Black Lives Matter movement has lifted the veil on the many real-life Lady Catherines, relying on their status as white women to get what they want.

As I will demonstrate, poking fun at mean girls takes away their bite.

I'd bet that despite our various failings, most of us aspire to be like Elizabeth Bennet, shielding Georgiana from the uncomfortable spotlight. We hope to be an Elinor Dashwood, able to keep another woman's secret, even if it hurts. We forgive featherbrained Louisa Musgrove's attention-seeking jump, even if we would like to bop her on the nose for being so foolish.

For in our heart of hearts, I'd bet that all of us have behaved like Austen's delightfully spiteful female characters at some point in our lives. Whether you refer to anthropology, psychology, or sociology, aspects of Austen's mean girls are present in all of us. Her six completed novels may not answer every question in life, but they shed light on the realities faced by both the good and the bad among us. Austen shows us an uncomfortable truth: the division between the two isn't always crystal clear.

The very first lesson of this book?

When in Doubt, Keep Calm and Read Jane Austen

Introduction

Other books are read; Austen's are devoured, digested,
and reinterpreted in the everyday lives of her readers.
—SUSANNAH CARSON

No one who had ever seen Jane Austen in her infancy would have supposed her destined to be one of the most important authors in English literature. Born the daughter of a clergyman in 1775, Austen was the second daughter and seventh child of eight. Her childhood home, the tiny village of Steventon, was in the middle of nowhere in the sleepy Hampshire countryside. She didn't have a special kind of upbringing. She and her sister received little formal education, and what travel she did enjoy was visiting friends and relatives. Nevertheless, the masterpieces produced from her sheltered, mostly rural life have earned unending devotion from fans worldwide. Austen herself would probably be astounded by her modern followers' fervent adoration and the millions of readers who find comfort in her six novels of family life.

The world will never really know Austen. After her death in 1817, the author's family made great efforts to portray her as a saintly, modest spinster, writing purely for amusement rather than ambition or money. Her beloved sister, Cassandra, moderated her memory by destroying an unknown number of her private letters. Of the estimated three thousand she wrote, fewer than two hundred remain. Those that survive hint at the tragic loss of countless delightfully snarky witticisms and insights that we will never experience.

The author of Austen's first biography, her nephew James Edward Austen-Leigh, established her Victorian reputation as sweet-tempered dear Aunt Jane. With terms like "full of moral rectitude," "correct taste," and "warm affections," Austen-Leigh patronizingly claimed Austen was very "careful not to meddle with matters which she did not thoroughly understand." His cloying descriptions don't match Austen's insightful portrayals of human behavior. Instead, they reflect later, Victorian, male expectations of female selflessness and submission.

It's hard to accept such a frilly, wide-eyed depiction of the woman capable of giving life to harpies like Lady Catherine de Bourgh and Fanny Dashwood. Still, the noble thing to do is forgive Austen-Leigh for his biographical transgressions. After all, he was only nineteen when his aunt died. Writing a biography about a long-dead spinster may not have been the best assignment for him. He certainly couldn't have predicted his aunt's current status as a feminist icon, printed on England's ten-pound note. Imagine his shock if he knew that, according to UK's *The Guardian* newspaper, *Pride and Prejudice* won out over the Judeo-Christian Bible in a World Book Day popularity poll.

Since Austen-Leigh, there have been countless Austen biographies. This book is not another. Instead, it is an investigation of intersections between the lives of Austen's female characters and her overwhelmingly female audience. I argue that both positive and negative relations between women are the true core of Austen's work.

My research began as a simple quest to understand why a female boss disliked me so much, and why her behavior reminded me of Jane Austen's mean girls. I was new on the job. Somewhat naively, I believed that the similarities in our age, education, and international background would be the solid basis for a healthy working relationship. Instead, I met with snippy bitching and posturing reminiscent of high school and its toxic combination of raging hormones and immaturity.

For some reason, I thought that behavior ended at the schoolyard gate.

I was wrong.

Not completely unsophisticated, I learned early in my corporate career not to automatically expect female solidarity. A particularly egregious example came while working on my HR qualification capstone project. Attempting to identify effective incentives to encourage more women managers to return to work after maternity leave, I examined compensation strategies in eighteen European subsidiaries. As a new mother myself, my findings were disheartening; benefits weren't the issue—attitudes were. One female head of HR shocked me to the core. During our interview, she defiantly told me that mothers have no role in management. Instead of outlining best-practice leave policies, she declared that mothers had no business in business. For her, it was clear. Childbirth meant the end of a woman's blind dedication to the company, and therefore, her career. Not surprisingly, there were no working mothers in her location. With her as a gatekeeper, no amount of home office policies or corporate daycare stipends would bring mothers back to such a hostile environment.

My literature review was equally disheartening. Titles like Lois Frankl's *Nice Girls Don't Get the Corner Office* and Gail Evans's *She Wins, You Win* showed me that female competition gets increasingly ruthless the nearer women get to the C-Suite. Since then, I have spoken to countless women who relate similar disappointing experiences. Several described leaving jobs, exhausted by intense bullying at the hands of female peers. One former colleague told of being edged out of a leadership role by a manager threatened by her expertise. Others were systematically left out of important after-hours meetings and communications, their once-confident selves seeming to shrink over time.

In real life, Austen's meanies seem to be everywhere. There's a streak of Lady Catherine de Bourgh in boardroom tokens. I sense the shadow of Mrs. Norris in a team of women who shunted one of their own into working from a converted broom closet, refusing to share space with her. There was a whiff of Emma Woodhouse in a colleague who admitted to rejecting a candidate she considered to be "too pretty."

Female gatekeepers, it seems, are both fact and fiction.

From the onset, I knew that understanding the mechanisms of female aggression wouldn't transform my situation. At best, I could learn how to manage my reaction to it. I wanted to be like Elizabeth Bennet, nonplussed by domineering Lady Catherine. I hoped to achieve the

Zen-like calm of Elinor Dashwood in the face of a disappointing turn of events.

Austen offers both answers and comfort in her spare descriptions of female behavior. Unlike her sensationalist contemporaries, she didn't rely on carriage chases, sexual abuse, or elaborate wedding scenes to make her mark on the world. Instead, the horrors Austen shares are remarkably like our own: a snub, some gossip, an ignored letter. She continues to give readers the gift of vicarious satisfaction in the behavior of mean girls like Caroline Bingley, Augusta Elton, and Mrs. Norris.

Not everyone agrees with me on this.

Austen has often been taken to task for her female characters' snarky behavior. Literature professor Julia Prewitt Brown explains, "Female authority figures in Austen have offended feminist critics . . . much in the way feminists today express embarrassment that women in positions of power behave just as badly as men."

A common complaint in historicist readings of Austen is that her stories only marginally—if at all—reflect the fact that she was writing during a period of almost constant war. However, Austen *does* specifically mention war twice, both concerning female aggression. First, the gullible Catherine Morland declares war on Isabella Thorpe; later, Emma Woodhouse considers herself in a "state of warfare" with Augusta Elton. For a female author whose lifetime was dominated by the repercussions of war (two brothers in the military and one relative guillotined in France), is it a coincidence that she used the term "war" to describe relations between women?

Austen's work is rife with cunning depictions of sneakily corrupt women, a trope employed since the beginning of recorded narrative. Greek mythology is full of spiteful women, often triggered by some idiot thing that Zeus did. The Bible is also full of female struggles, like Sarah using, then casting away Hagar. Shakespeare tells of sisters Regan and Goneril fighting for Edmund. History tells us that Queen Elizabeth I and Mary Stuart hated each other, leading to Mary's decapitation at her cousin's order. More recently, the British press propagated the rumor that the late Queen Elizabeth snubbed and bullied her daughter-in-law, Princess Diana. Of course, Catherine Middleton and Meghan Markle "cannot get along."

It starts early. Children's literature is overflowing with catfights. As recently as 2008, a study by psychologists S. M. Coyne and E. Whitehead found that indirect aggression among female characters was present in 100 percent of animated Disney movies and 90 percent of children's media overall. It's not new. The original Cinderella's stepsisters would rather chop off their toes than see her wed a prince. Snow White's jealous stepmother tried to have her murdered. A witch put Princess Aurora into a coma, angry for not being invited to a party. Even after the passage of decades, I still remember my visceral responses to canonical descriptions of adolescent female aggression. I was shocked when Amy March burned Jo's draft novel, disgusted at Josie Pye's cruel attacks on Anne Shirley, and horrified by Nelly Olsen's pettiness toward Laura Ingalls.

Unfortunately, these representations have a basis in actual social interaction. In the 1980s, anthropologists aggregated over a century's worth of findings on 137 societies from across the globe, identifying female aggression *in every single one*. Not only do women aggress, they found, but they also seem more likely to direct their anger at other women than men.

Despite a societal reluctance to scrutinize the phenomenon, female aggression is something that most women encounter in their lives. As a Hollywood trope, it sells. How else to explain the mass appeal of the 2004 film *Mean Girls*, revived in 2018 as a musical, and the 1988 black comedy *Heathers*, transformed into a television series in 2017?

Surprisingly, this stealthy type of aggression has only recently received attention in the social sciences and even less consideration in Austen scholarship. The phenomenon of female misogyny is everywhere and yet remains bewildering, going against cultural norms, which still expect women to be "sugar and spice and everything nice."

If female aggression is such a disappointing topic, then why do we seek it out as consumers? Since Aristotle's *Poetics*, scholars have tried to explain the attraction of certain narratives. Many, under the name

Reader Response Theory, suggest that we feel like we "know" some fictional characters because of what we bring to the act of reading. Readers aren't blank slates. According to their thinking, I was predisposed to identify with Austen's scenes of female power relations at that time in my life. After all, my livelihood was threatened by the actions of a female boss.

Professor of English Susan Ostrov Weisser argues that fictional mean girls are instrumental, rendering "a quick dose of terrible discomfort within a safe frame that provides an expectation of ultimate comfort and mastery of anxiety." For Weisser, depictions of female aggression vex narratives, rendering "the world of love . . . all the more gratifying when restored." It's like adding a bit of salt to a sweet recipe; the contrast enhances the flavor. It's hard to imagine what *Pride and Prejudice* would be without a Caroline Bingley to get in the way. Without Lucy Steele, *Sense and Sensibility* would be a short story, and the lack of Mrs. Norris would render *Mansfield Park* and Fanny Price even more saccharine than they already are.

Was it just me? I asked the Janeite community how they saw things. It wasn't hard finding fans to share their experiences. We are a communicative bunch. I surveyed members of various analog and digital Austen fan groups, asking what they thought of Austen's good and bad girls.

Austen adoration seems to know no age barriers; respondents ranged from teenagers to septuagenarians. While most came from Western countries, I also had respondents from Asia, Africa, and South America. Of the 397 people who took part, 98 percent identified as female. Half claimed to have read all of Austen's novels at least once, with over a quarter having read them all at least twice. Unsurprisingly, most reported finding Austen's female characters realistic and relatable.

Beyond the numbers, their comments spoke directly to my Janeite heart. "Her characters seem like real people to me," wrote one. Another confessed that "the vast majority of her characters are so well drawn that it is possible to find points of similarity between myself and most of them, even if I don't want to!" One revealed that "after countless readings, I still cry with Elinor, Elizabeth, and Anne." Another related getting "angry on Fanny's behalf," while one claimed, "I knew a Mrs. Elton, once." Two admitted that, at one point in their lives, "I *was* Lizzie."

Even more intriguing were the statements about Austen's mean girls, which included heated denunciations from "Lucy Steele makes my skin crawl," "Mrs. Norris is the worst of the worst," and "Mrs. Norris can go straight to hell." Many considered Austen's antagonists more realistic than her good girls. One claimed, "I've seen the behaviors of her female villains in everyday life. I've seen less of the strengths of her good characters." Another confessed, "I'm quite a pessimist and find negative characters to be more believable," and "Austen's unlikeable characters . . . ? The world is full of them!" Some participants seemed to revel in hating specific personalities, with statements including, "of course, while I find some of these characters extremely dislikable, I love them" and expressions of "enjoying a character for their awfulness."

One thing that I hadn't reckoned with was heroine backlash. Many participants chimed in that moral righteousness was far less believable than bitchiness. One woman related, "I think I find the more flawed/devious characters realistic because the heroines are all so good." Another remarked, "Elinor is just . . . a little too good to be true sometimes." Prissy Fanny Price was considered the least realistic of the bunch. One wrote, "Fanny Price is just too perfect for reality," another "I really can't with Fanny Price," and "I feel like I've known all of these people in real life (except maybe for Fanny)." At the same time, many expressed understanding, if not approval, of Austen's mean girls. For example, while making one reader's "skin crawl," Lucy Steele is pardoned by others as merely "insecure and jealous." Instead of anger, Isabella Thorpe and Caroline Bingley arouse pity. One reader sums it up: "you know these characters because you've interacted with them in real life."

I've encountered both recognition and resistance discussing my research with other women. Almost every female researcher of intra-gender aggression repeats this sentiment, often feeling pressure from other women to portray their lives as harmonious. Instead, women across the globe relate experiencing failures in female solidarity daily. In their work on the subject, *Feminist Nightmares: Women at Odds: Feminism and the Problems of Sisterhood*, professors Susan Ostrov Weisser and Jennifer Fleischner argue that "as daughters, mothers, wives, lovers, friends, and workers," women expect others of their sex to "lift us above the tensions of living in a world of multifarious, interlocking oppressions." Weisser and Fleischner warn that the "insistence on sisterhood as a characteristic (rather than ideal) trait of women" only increases the problem.

Instead of evading discussion, they recommend that women face it head-on.

Ironically, my research into aggression among women has brought me closer to many female colleagues and friends. Instead of denying its existence, almost all of them shared their own stories of hurt and frustration. This simple act was a relief. Female aggression, often hidden in glances, exclusion, and gossip, seldom marks its victims. Instead, it leaves them feeling lost and alone. Connecting these behaviors back to the world of Jane Austen reveals that things haven't changed that much for women in this world.

The lesson for me?

It's Up to Every One of Us to Do Our Part to Change Things

This book is my attempt.

Part I

YOUTHFUL INDISCRETIONS

Caroline Bingley

Angry People Are Not Always Wise

The world is profoundly scared of single women; they are loose cannons, the uncontrollable variable, hormones and pheromones afloat and adrift; much more frightening than the extra man at a dinner party, they are the piece that can change the status quo, upset the balance, break up families.

—ELIZABETH WURZEL

Few women enjoy a straight trajectory in life and love. It often seems that some*one* or some*thing* is getting in the way. Often, that hurdle is our own personal Caroline Bingley. For many who come to Austen through *Pride and Prejudice* film adaptations, Caroline's their gateway bonneted bitch. On paper and film, she's easy to hate. Lording over Lizzie Bennet from her soapbox built of wealth, education, and social connections, Caroline does her best to undermine Elizabeth's chances of marrying Mr. Darcy.

Reading and re-reading *Pride and Prejudice* over the decades, I've come to realize that Caroline is everywhere—even in me. She represents the worst of us, having much, yet denying others a part of it. Of course, Caroline doesn't physically hurt the Bennet girls (unless you are reading *Pride and Prejudice and Zombies*). Instead, she uses indirect ways of causing harm, delineated with such a light hand that we can recognize them anywhere.

Simply put, Caroline is a well-known nuisance.

Let's begin with what women were fighting for in *Pride and Prejudice*: a suitable mate. It's clear from the very first line, "It is a truth universally acknowledged that a single man in possession of a good fortune must be in want of a wife." Within just a few pages, the Bennet girls are established as career manhunters with a weak, disinterested father and hypochondriacal mother.

It's hard to blame them. Without any brothers, the five Bennet sisters have only a meager inheritance. To make matters worse, they and their mother will lose their home as soon as their father passes. Whatever future security they hope to have, it's up to them to find it.

Oddly, their parents haven't prepared them for this role. Mr. and Mrs. Bennet's mistaken reliance on producing a male heir means that none of their daughters had formal schooling or even a level-headed governess. Only the dowdy middle daughter, pianoforte-playing Mary, can display any of the traditional accomplishments expected of their social set (and poorly at that).

With all of this to contend with, it's no wonder that the sudden influx of handsome, young militiamen in the neighborhood sparks joy in their hearts. The arrival of Charles Bingley, a hot new bonus bachelor with enough cash to rent swish Netherfield Hall, ups the odds that a Bennet girl will find a match.

FEMALE AGGRESSION IS SUBTLE

History tells us that competition for suitable men was fierce when the novel was written, and the first hint of mean girl behavior revolves around the fight for a mate. The Bennet girls are troubled to learn that Mr. Bingley won't come alone to Meryton. Instead, he is rumored to be bringing "such a number of ladies." With so few men to choose from, the addition of even one marriageable woman into their tiny community spelled trouble. Charles and the militia are met with open arms; ladies are not.

The first encounter between Bingley's sisters and the Bennet girls doesn't bode well. Elizabeth quickly finds fault. After the briefest of contacts, she determines them to be "proud and conceited" and "was very little disposed to approve of them." As the sister of a wealthy man, Caroline Bingley enjoys a vastly different social status than Elizabeth, and it shows in her clothing and mannerisms. Theoretically, she should be less desperate to marry than the Bennets, who were victims of an entail on their family home. However, all women in the early 1800s were nonpersons in the eyes of the law. Unable to own property, they were subject to the decisions of their husbands or male relatives, whose status had increased in the previous century.

In Regency Britain, almost constant wars on the continent and in the colonies significantly reduced England's male population. Historian Lawrence Stone finds that the proportion of spinsters among upper-class daughters rose from just 5 percent to 25 percent during the century before. Periodicals of the day are filled with essays asking, "What shall we do with the old maids?" as increasing numbers of highly born ladies remained unmarried.

In the nineteenth century, growing industrialization and men rising in military ranks rendered the marriage market even more dire. Wealth was no longer linked entirely to property ownership, making things difficult for the landed gentry's daughters. Newly wealthy fathers of industry like Caroline's could afford monetary dowries for their girls, making them more attractive as mates. Ancient landowners like Mr. Bennet couldn't keep up, meaning their daughters became less enticing prospects. Instead of traditional alliances with girls from the neighboring gentry, male heirs could shop for wives among the nouveau riche. Eligible bachelors became more and more valuable, while unmarried women became expendable.

It's also important to understand that the notion of marrying for love was only just beginning to take hold in society when Austen wrote *Pride and Prejudice*. Historically, Stone explains, weddings were business transactions between fathers, not the happy endings we now expect. Regency readers would have been acutely aware of this, and much less likely to judge Charlotte Lucas's prudent union with Mr. Collins than today's idealistic singles.

Realistically, it's impossible to know just how many marriages at the time were based on similar grounds. For many men, wives were regarded as breeders, whether of heirs or simply additional labor. It's heartbreaking to realize how few of our Regency counterparts may have had real love in their lives. Whether straight, lesbian, queer, trans—we can only hope that some of our foremothers could claim their true sexuality and consent.

Unfortunately, choosing a career instead of marriage wasn't a viable option, especially for the Bingleys' social set. Like Caroline (and Austen herself), the lesser gentry's spinsters had no choice but to trail their male relatives, often earning their keep through household management or childcare. Their mere presence in a home suggested that the family wasn't affluent enough to marry them off. According to Stone, the only women who *could* afford to remain single were wealthy heiresses. His work shows that only a very few ladies from extremely well-to-do families could establish comfortable lives independently. Of course, this didn't mean that they pursued a vocation. Instead, it meant that they could afford a life filled with correspondence, paid companions, and visits to family and friends.

As the daughter of a clergyman, Austen knew firsthand that a father's death meant his income's disappearance. After he passed, Austen and her mother and sister moved to ever-shrinking rented accommodations before finally taking up residence at a cottage owned by a brother. Many women weren't as lucky, having no sons or brothers to save them. Regency newspapers like *The Bath Chronicle* were full of heartbreaking calls for charity as widows and orphans found themselves in financial difficulties.

Less fortunate old maids and widows relied on the generosity of friends and neighbors. In this, Caroline was at an advantage. Although her parents were dead, her inheritance made her slightly more independent. Nevertheless, like Lizzy, Caroline couldn't strike out on her own.

Instead, she was forced to follow her married sister or brother wherever they chose to take her.

The burden of spinsterhood wasn't only financial but social as well. Unmarried women carried a stigma, and there seemed to be no reluctance to name and shame them. British historian and satirist Richard Carlisle wrote in 1858 that it could "hardly have escaped the notice of anyone that women who have never had sexual commerce begin to droop when about twenty-five years of age." To add insult to injury, Carlisle declared that "their forms degenerate" and "their features sink." With such opinions circulating in society, it is hardly surprising that women did what they could to avoid them.

The young women of *Pride and Prejudice* know very well what is required. While the eyes of Meryton's mothers were on her sunny-tempered brother, Caroline angles for his close friend, Fitzwilliam Darcy. Well-heeled and educated, Mr. Darcy owns a significant estate in the north of England. Few modern readers can immediately translate the value of his ten thousand pounds a year, yet they understand Mrs. Bennet's instant evaluation of him as a highly desirable son-in-law. On top of that, Caroline's actions single him out as a catch. We see her marking him as her territory through comments, compliments, and turns about the room.

THE PRESSURE TO PAIR HASN'T STOPPED

Today, of course, marriage isn't the only career choice for women, yet the parallels remain. Finding "the one" feels like an important milestone in personal fulfillment for many people. Wanting to be loved is human, and many women aspire to a monogamous relationship as well as motherhood.

According to American educator Rosalind Wiseman, this sentiment starts early. Based on years of working with girls in US schools, Wiseman finds that being part of a couple is so socially expected that, "at some point, most girls will lie, connive, or backstab to get the boy they want." Wiseman finds that being a part of a couple represents a crucial validation for young women. Having a romantic partner offers them a sense of belonging and increases a girl's social standing amongst her peers. Objectively speaking, it's a reality not much different from the one Austen describes.

Even after high school, Western society's obsession with women pairing off isn't a private affair. Preoccupation with relationship status seems ubiquitous, from pointed questions at family dinners to fashion magazines focused on pleasing a man. Fascination with coupling is everywhere. Why else would millions of global viewers tune in for the wedding of Prince Harry and Meghan Markle? How else to explain the bizarre acceptance of shows like *The Bachelor*? Since its introduction in 2002, audiences have endorsed its format of a single man concurrently dating twenty-five different women, eventually selecting one to marry. The trend hasn't weakened; Netflix has introduced three separate English-language dating programs in the past few years: *Dating Around*, *Love Is Blind*, and *Too Hot to Handle*.

For years, heterosexual Western women have been fed the narrative that finding a husband is like winning the lottery. Gen-X-ers may remember the infamous *Newsweek* article on modern marriage, which ran in the late eighties. Its authors claimed that women over age forty are more likely to get killed by terrorists than find a husband. While the assertion has since been debunked, it began a cultural uproar that has yet to cease. It inspired countless Hollywood rom-coms and self-help books. The trope was an international bestseller in Candace Bushnell's *Sex and the City* columns and television programs and Helen Fielding's *Bridget Jones's Diary* series. Finding an eligible partner was portrayed as beating the odds, a theme still trotted out each Christmas in a host of saccharine Hallmark movies.

While the *Newsweek* premise is patently untrue, its message has lingered. *The Atlantic*'s Megan Garber assesses that its sense of acute anxiety remains "oddly fresh." She explains that its motto, "panic, ladies," lives on "in every current news story about the difficulty educated women face in the 'marriage market.'" For Garber and many other women, the sentiment intensifies with "every blithe reference to the 'biological clock,' and indeed in every piece of media that gazes upon women's bodies and sees, in their fleshy fallibility, some form of social determinism." These sentiments don't seem much different than those of Austen's world.

To make things even more complicated, many women continue to feel pressure to marry "up," a practice known as hypergamy. For women, this "right" kind of union represents an increase in social or economic status. Remarkably, this message has carried on despite advances in women's rights, educational levels, and representation in the workforce.

Whether unconscious or conscious, the yearning for hypergamy persists. According to data scientist Bradford Tuckfield, hypergamy remains both expected and challenging in many parts of the world. As the number of well-educated, financially stable women is growing, the pool of men whose training and earnings are superior to theirs isn't. Many independent, successful heterosexual Western women with advanced degrees find it challenging to meet a guy with equal social status, much less more.

Further afield, cultural norms and family planning policies have resulted in a shortage of women in some places. Demographic records indicate that in any population, for every 100 female births, there should be up to 105 males born. According to the World Health Organization, the now amended One-Child Policy forced families in China to make choices. As a result, the ratio of boys to girls born there reached 120 to 100 for several decades. Similar statistics are found in India, where sex-selective abortions in some places allow families to ensure they have a baby boy.

There are consequences. China's male-only children are now coming of age, and the skewed sex ratio is suddenly a problem. In rural areas, it's become a seller's market. Bride prices, or the amount expected to be paid by a prospective groom to his future wife's parents, are rising. Men of lesser means remain single or look to other countries for mates within their financial reach. Disturbingly, these "cheaper alternatives" don't always have a choice in the matter.

Different types of hypergamy are found in the West, where some men resent changes in traditional gender roles. In "reverse hypergamy," these guys aim to marry "down," looking to mail-order brides from developing countries to fulfill their antiquated expectations. As a feminist, I find their misogynistic rhetoric revolting. Even more disturbing are global reports of the brutality and violence that many of these women experience once leaving their homelands.

It's impossible to look inside anyone else's marriage. One can only hope that some of these unions are as happy as any between consenting adults *can* be. As a privileged white Western woman, I can't begin to understand these brides' decisions, nor the economic and psychological impact on them and their families. The same sentiment haunts me each time I read Charlotte Lucas's story and imagine how many women in our civilization have had to make do, leading lives without knowing personal or sexual fulfillment.

Like Caroline Bingley, I've had my doubts. In my twenties, my friends were pairing up, and being unattached felt like being left out of the natural progression of life. Like so many panicked nineties singles, I bought a copy of Ellen Fein and Sherrie Schneider's bestseller, *The Rules: Time-Tested Secrets for Capturing the Heart of Mr. Right*. According to them, modern dating is just as rule-laden as in the Regency. Although my dad didn't have to ride to Netherfield to introduce himself on my behalf, Fein and Schneider told me not to ask a man to dance. I *could* dance more than twice with a man without scandal, but I shouldn't call him on the phone. Fein and Schneider advised me that the appearance of availability was a surefire way to kill a man's interest. Just as Austen showed her contemporaries, *The Rules* taught me the kind of husband that showing enthusiasm brought a woman: a Mr. Collins or a Wickham.

The Rules landed quickly and quietly in my recycling bin.

Eventually, I did find Mr. Right. He doesn't look much like Mr. Darcy, but he does like to dance. As a feminist, I'd like to believe I married him solely for his great smile and brilliant mind. But as a mother, I recognize the powerful role financial resources and employment prospects have in everyday family life.

PARENTAL INVESTMENT IMPACTS JUST ABOUT EVERYTHING

Before you call me mercenary, let me explain. According to biologist Robert Trivers, assets represent more to women than to men when selecting a mate. It isn't that we are more superficial. Trivers's assertion is based on fundamental differences in what he calls "parental investment."

In the twenty-first century, Western men play a much more significant role in childrearing than in the past. Nevertheless, biology has its limits. Despite advances in gender equality and Western rejection of archaic parenting roles, mothers are more involved in their child's first year of life than fathers. Simply put, gestation and lactation remain (in general) the remit of women. A healthy woman can physically produce and nurse only one or two babies in a given year. In the process, our bodies change drastically, even costing some of us our lives. In contrast, a man could (theoretically) father hundreds, if not thousands of babies in the forty weeks between a single child's conception and birth. (Gentlemen, do not try this at home.)

In this light, Austen's description of Caroline's behavior makes sense. Mate selection is essential in ensuring the viability of her future children. Caroline's genetic material is present in her brother's reproductive choices, and she is invested in protecting his DNA as well as her own. Considering the questionable behavior displayed by the entire Bennet family, it isn't entirely unreasonable for Caroline to doubt the suitability of his attachment to Jane.

Caroline Bingley, a fictional, wealthy Regency woman with little personal agency, is sadly reminiscent of any number of my suburban peers. Like her, most of us enjoy what many would call a privileged life, and few of us have known hunger or worried about having a place to sleep at night. Nevertheless, like Caroline, we can be ruthless creatures.

As the title suggests, judgment plays a pivotal role in *Pride and Prejudice*, even beyond Elizabeth and Darcy's immediate evaluation of one another. Relations between the Bennet and Bingley ladies begin positively as soon as the Bennets learn that only one of the newcomers is single. Mrs. Bennet declares Caroline and her sister "charming," judging both to be "fine women," but only as long as they admire and distinguish Jane. The regard was mutually conditional. Although "the mother was found to be intolerable, and the younger sisters not worth speaking to," Bingley's sisters enjoy Jane's company. In turn, Elizabeth views them skeptically, detecting "superciliousness in their treatment of everybody, hardly excepting even her sister, and could not like them."

JUDGING OTHERS ISN'T NICE, BUT IT'S NORMAL

Austen signposts Caroline and Lizzy's hyperawareness of each other. The prestige differentials may differ from today, but modern readers understand the sentiment. Anyone who has suffered the indignities of simply wearing the "wrong" kind of clothing, having the "wrong" type of body, or having an empty bank account can sense what Caroline's sniggers mean. To Mrs. Bennet, dining "with four-and-twenty families" denotes privilege. To the Bingley sisters, it's a joke. Likewise, Austen could have chosen any London street or neighborhood to locate the Gardiners. Her selection of Cheapside acts as shorthand, ensuring that even readers unfamiliar with England's capital understand the address as less than fashionable. Ironically, the address in Gracechurch Street places them within the Square Mile, currently vying with Manhattan to be the world's financial capital, a stone's throw from the ultra-trendy, gentrified Shoreditch.

Caroline and her sister live in a traditionally elite part of town. Unlike the Bennets, they were used to "associating with people of rank," feeling "entitled to think well of themselves, and meanly of others." They have no problem flaunting their wealth and privileged upbringing, conveniently forgetting that it was earned (gasp!) through trade. In contrast to the pastoral Bennet family, the more sophisticated Bingley sisters are described as experienced musicians, displaying "an air of decided fashion" and having fortunes at their disposal. The Bennet sisters could only afford a season in Brighton when accompanying an affluent friend.

No wonder Elizabeth has no patience for Caroline.

According to anthropologist Donald Brown, we humans are materialistic, and every known language has a concept of possession. As a species, we judge others, often out of a fundamental need to belong. By classifying ourselves and others into imaginary categories, we establish in-groups and out-groups, learning where we fit. Belonging to a group provides us with a sense of identity and self-esteem.

The Bennet sisters are part of several. Together, they are kin. As individuals, they represent young, unmarried women from Meryton. Although technically the daughters of a gentleman, their uncertain futures separate them from the Bingley ladies. Feelings of connection between the Bennet and Bingley sisters are fluid; Caroline identifies with Jane as young and single, resulting in an invitation to dinner and gossip at Netherfield. The similarities end there.

The next day, Elizabeth's bedraggled appearance on their doorstep proves to the Bingley sisters that the Bennets are rural and uncouth and miss no opportunity to comment on it. Caroline denigrates not only Elizabeth's dirty hem but her entirety. After supper, she and Louisa indulge "their mirth for some time at the expense of their dear friend's [Jane's] vulgar relations." Things worsen when Caroline senses that Darcy is no longer averse to Elizabeth's cute figure and teasing ways. When Caroline catches him eying their guest, she prods him to join her malicious scrutiny. She proposes "you are considering how insupportable it would be to pass many evenings in this manner—in such society." Continuing, she laments "the insipidity, and yet the noise—the nothingness, and yet the self-importance of all those people!"

Her ploy backfires. Caroline is "all astonishment" to learn that instead of mocking Elizabeth, Darcy was "meditating" on her "fine eyes." Playfully attempting to horrify him, Caroline pushes the point. "How long has she been such a favorite?" she asks, adding, "and pray, when am I to wish you joy?" Not hearing the strong denial she expected, Miss Bingley continues to provoke, declaring that he will have a charming mother-in-law, who will always be at Pemberley with him and his bride. Ever composed, Darcy listens to her nonsense with "perfect indifference" as she "chose to entertain herself in this manner." She takes his silence as a sign that "all was safe," continuing to chatter on and on.

It's passages like these where Austen is at her most bewitching. She gets her readers to judge her characters for being judgmental with just a few words. Without a second thought, we do her bidding. Instead of wanting to be more like the fashionable Bingley ladies, we all want to be muddy and sniffy Bennets. Who cares about a bit of dirt? Reading Caroline's pettiness, we instantly take Elizabeth's side. We admire her disinterest in Caroline's appraisals. After all, she traipses over hill and dale, through mud and meadow to ensure her beloved sister's comfort. What could be wrong with that?

Later in the story, Austen manages to seduce us into applauding Elizabeth's egalitarian willingness to take the word of a steward's son on the value of his honest-looking face. It takes a while to learn that both her infatuation and our assumptions aren't all that noble. After all, it only took Elizabeth a minute to determine that she "could not like" Caroline and one evening to know that Mr. Darcy was the last person on Earth whom she could marry. At the end of the story, it's hard to know who's the kettle and who's the pot.

In his work on Austen and Social Identity Theory, literary scholar Matt Lorenz spotlights the hypocrisy of Austen's female characters. He points out that the Bingley sisters are pleasant to Elizabeth when she's around, only beginning to abuse her when she leaves the room. Their assault isn't a secret; they mean for Darcy to hear every word. When he fails to react, Caroline doubles down, drawing attention to Elizabeth's every flaw. In a half-whisper, she intimates, "I am afraid, Mr. Darcy . . . that this adventure has rather affected your admiration" of Elizabeth's "fine eyes."

His declaration of their being "brightened by the exercise" is essential information for both Caroline and the reader. Not only do we learn that Darcy is attracted to Elizabeth, but we also understand that Caroline will do anything within her minimal power to change this. Not satisfied with his response, Caroline attacks Elizabeth's behavior instead. She fantasies further on their imminent match, telling Darcy that he should "endeavor to check that little something, bordering on conceit and impertinence, which your lady possesses."

Revealing the self-awareness of a doorknob, Caroline declares Elizabeth to be "one of those young ladies who seek to recommend themselves to the other sex by undervaluing their own." Caroline doesn't realize she is doing *the exact thing* that she criticizes Elizabeth for, calling it "a paltry device, a very mean art." Provocatively, Lorenz points out that Caroline isn't so very different from Elizabeth's mother, Mrs. Bennet. Neither approves of this young woman who refuses to conform to their expectations of feminine behavior. Caroline can't understand Elizabeth's attachment to the low-born Wickham, and Mrs. Bennet can't fathom her daughter's refusal of Mr. Collins. Neither can comprehend traipsing three miles through the soggy countryside to attend to a sister. Except for the difference in their fortunes and "Miss Bingley's greater vigilance about the propriety of her behavior," Lorenz finds little disparity between the two. Lorenz considers both to be petty and vindictive, declaring any attractive woman of marriageable age to be their sworn enemy.

Both share a tendency to gossip, using language to inform or misinform, entertain, and insult. It's a verbal give and take that establishes a sense of superiority and intimacy, reinforcing group identity to include as well as exclude. As literary scholars Patricia Meyer Spacks and Blakey Vermeule point out, Austen's novels are rife with it. Only the practically perfect Jane hesitates to share hot information in *Pride and Prejudice*. In contrast, Caroline is incredibly free with her insinuations about Elizabeth and her family, sharing her catalog of perceived faults with anyone who will listen.

In evolutionary psychological terms, gossip is a way to manage group relations and establish a sense of community by disseminating information such as shared values and objectives. Austen uses the tittle-tattle after Netherfield dinners to highlight her heroine's obstacles. Our opinions about Darcy slowly change as he sees through Caroline's machinations, even telling her that what she is doing is incredibly unattractive. He specifically states that he finds "meanness in all the arts which ladies sometimes condescend to employ for captivation," determining that cunning of the sort to be despicable.

Caroline fails to grasp the message. At most, Darcy's words leave her nervous and "not so entirely satisfied." She regroups, enlisting her sister in badmouthing the family, beginning with their guest. Mrs. Hurst condescends to "have an excessive regard for Miss Jane Bennet" while predicting that she had little hope for a good match with such wretched parents and low connections. Their comments are clear warnings that the Bennet girls are *not* appropriate wife material. Through them, Austen outlines the expectations for female behavior in the Bingleys' social set and that Elizabeth does not meet the mark.

Modern women are used to this; psychologist Tracy Vaillancourt explains that "in human females, sexual selection has given rise to two strategies—self-promotion and the derogation of rivals," both of which Caroline amply demonstrates. In her wonderfully titled article, "Tripping the Prom Queen," Vaillancourt surveyed over one thousand female university students. Over 80 percent admitted to being bitchy toward other girls, with 94 percent confessing to talk behind another girl's back. Their main targets? The girls they saw as most threatening to their goals.

For Caroline, that person is Elizabeth Bennet.

Admittedly, Lizzy's muddy frock wasn't the problem, but her "fine eyes" certainly were. Caroline's petty derisions after dinner are meant to besmirch Elizabeth, whom she sees as a rival. The phenomenon is supported by social scientist Tania Reynolds and her colleagues. In five separate studies, they demonstrate that women selectively share (or hide) reputation-relevant information, especially about women they find too attractive or too provocatively dressed. They also find that the more competitive a woman is, the more likely she will broadcast damaging reports about another. Less beautiful women aren't worth the bother; they are simply ignored.

Despite all the negativity, Reynolds and her colleagues found gossip positive in certain circumstances. No matter if the subject is good or bad, gossip circulates information. It's a form of sharing, regardless of our affection or animosity toward the person being discussed. In *Why Do We Care about Literary Characters*, Vermeule suggests that humans need gossip, and we are drawn to fictional characters by our need to know about other people. In exchange for our attention, fiction "pays us back with large doses of really juicy social information." Growing up as someone who never had the right kinds of clothes and tended to be muddier than not, reading about well-dressed Caroline Bingley's many insecurities was reassuring. In my love-starved teenage heart, these scenes of petty, one-way rivalry gave me hope that someone, someday, may find my eyes "fine."

Vermeule underscores this, concluding that novels offer a safe way to learn about the world around us. By suspending our disbelief, we can examine things that "would be too costly, dangerous, and difficult to extract from the world on our own." For Vermeule, readers participate in the kinds of novels that show us "the deep truth about people's intentions." If we're lucky, we can even discover things about ourselves. Gossip, Vermeule proposes, is the very reason we read Austen.

Of course, gossip is just one of many universal strategies to manipulate those around us. Economist and political scientist Michael Chwe explores this in *Jane Austen: Game Theorist*. Citing Mrs. Bennet's calculated dispatch of Jane on horseback to Charlotte taking Mr. Collins under her wing, Chwe shows Austen as a natural strategist. He claims that Austen knew the tactics needed to win the mating game well. In contrast, Mrs. Hurst and Caroline are a bit slow on the uptake, underestimating Mrs. Bennet's drive to get her daughters married off. Their invitation to Jane appears incredibly naive in retrospect. Mrs. Bennet earns bonus points when Jane is forced to spend the night due to bad weather, and she levels up quickly when Jane falls ill from exposure. In one move, plus a sniffy nose and a cough, Mrs. Bennet gets her eldest daughter into a Bingley bed. Who knows how many points she earns when Lizzie joins Jane there?

Caroline is simply no match for the Bennet brigade. Miserably unable to control the situation, she is left floundering. In the evenings, she fusses over Darcy, paying him useless compliments "on the evenness of his lines, or on the length of his letter"—patter hardly likely to incite fiery passion. Alternatively, she becomes a bibliophile's nightmare, gawping at "Mr. Darcy's progress through his book," instead of sitting down and quietly reading her own. In desperation, she turns to Elizabeth, who is quite able to entertain herself. Miss Bingley calls for Lizzie to join her in "a turn about the room." Finally, by pairing up with her rival, "Miss Bingley succeeded . . . in the real object of her civility; Mr. Darcy looked up."

It was an empty victory. The Bennet girls' mere existence destroys Caroline and Mrs. Hurst's plans for a quiet country holiday. Instead of a rural retreat, they are forced to watch Darcy grow besotted with Elizabeth, and their brother fall head over heels for Jane. As quickly as they can, Caroline and Louisa take matters into their own hands, convincing Charles to remove to London. Under their encouragement, what should have been a short business trip lengthens indefinitely.

Caroline informs Jane of their departure, intimating that their friendship wouldn't suffer by the distance. "I do not pretend to regret anything I shall leave in Hertfordshire, except your society, my dearest friend," the hypocritical Caroline assures. Slowly and quietly, she drives a dagger into Jane's unsuspecting heart. "I do not know whether I ever before mentioned to you my feelings on this subject," Caroline intimates, "but I will not leave the country without confiding them." The secret? She and Louisa have already selected a wife for their brother: Georgiana Darcy, whom Caroline regards as having no "equal for beauty, elegance, and accomplishments." Caroline announces, Georgiana's "relations all wish the connection as much as his."

Reaching for the salt, Caroline beseeches Jane for agreement. "With all these circumstances to favor an attachment, and nothing to prevent it," she implores, "am I wrong, my dearest Jane, in indulging the hope of an event which will secure the happiness of so many?" Even good-hearted Jane is wise enough to understand her meaning. "Is it not clear enough? Does it not expressly declare that Caroline neither expects nor wishes me to be her sister; that she is perfectly convinced of her brother's indifference?" Naively, Jane translates Caroline's intention as being "(most kindly!) to put me on my guard," imploring, "can there be any other opinion on the subject?"

Elizabeth (and I bet most of us) interprets the letter more skeptically, understanding it as manipulation. Elizabeth assures Jane that "Miss Bingley sees that her brother is in love with you and wants him to marry Miss Darcy." She accurately predicts that Caroline wants to keep him in London to nip the attraction in the bud. "No one who has ever seen you together can doubt his affection," Elizabeth declares. "Miss Bingley, I am sure, cannot. She is not such a simpleton. Could she have seen half as much love in Mr. Darcy for herself, she would have ordered her wedding clothes."

Pragmatic Elizabeth knows that the Bennets aren't part of the Bingley sisters' in-group. "The case is this," she says. "We are not rich enough or grand enough for them." Despite Lizzie's best efforts, Caroline's arrow has hit its mark. The compliant, heartsick Jane queries, "but, my dear sister, can I be happy, even supposing the best, in accepting a man whose sisters and friends are all wishing him to marry elsewhere?"

Always on Jane's side, Elizabeth convinces her to follow Bingley to the capital. After all, she could count on Regency manners and the principle of reciprocity to work on her behalf. Austen teaches twenty-first-century women this from the beginning: one call or letter begets one in return. What could go wrong?

RECIPROCITY IS EXPECTED

According to Donald Brown, reciprocity is a part of all cultures—group survival depends on it. In Regency England, custom dictated that women of Austen's social class follow a kind of politeness ping-pong.

One lady paid respects to another with a call. If the person was home, they conversed for at least fifteen minutes. If not at home, the visitor left her card. A calling card or letter was like an opening volley; the recipient was expected to react promptly. Regency social calls could open—or close—social ties.

Making and returning calls may seem old-fashioned to modern readers, but small children know the trade-off instinctively. If I invite you to my birthday party, I better damn well be guaranteed a spot at yours.

In more adult terms, Brown describes such codified forms of give-and-take as the cornerstone of group life, often with strong moral feelings attached to them. Assured of a socially dictated response, Jane blithely informs Bingley's sisters of her arrival in town, and their failure to respond immediately sets off alarm bells.

Jane couldn't imagine that the Bingley sisters would cut her off so completely. Always positive, she pays them a call. Baffled by their icy reception, Jane continues to make allowances for them. Writing to Elizabeth, she relates "I did not think Caroline in spirits," marveling at the reproach she received for not letting the Bingleys know that she was in London. No matter what game Caroline played, social reciprocity meant returning Jane's visit in good time. While she *could* pretend not to have received a letter, the presence of a real, live Jane in her drawing-room was harder to ignore. Still, Caroline made the best use of her power by turning the timing of her call into an insult.

Sanguine Jane predicted that it would be prompt. Four long weeks passed before Caroline presented herself in Gracechurch Street. When she finally showed up, she made it clear that "she had no pleasure in it," behavior so blatant that even kindhearted Jane couldn't ignore it. Finally, the eldest Bennet daughter conceded, admitting Miss Bingley's true nature. Her snub of Jane had a different tone from her hatred of Elizabeth. For Caroline, Jane was a welcome diversion at a rural retreat. In contrast, Elizabeth is a threat, best never to be seen again.

COMPETITION BREEDS CONTEMPT

It's easy to imagine Caroline's horror when the fine-eyed Elizabeth pops up out of the blue at Pemberley. Readers recognize the character's jealousy early in the novel, even if Caroline and Elizabeth don't realize it until much later. Finally understanding the enormity of Darcy's fortune while touring the estate, Lizzie wasn't surprised to find herself being closely watched by Miss Bingley as she and her relatives were welcomed into the stately home.

According to Brown, the rivalry between two people over a third is also part of every known society. It arises from the simple fact that most humans are sexual beings, and sexual attraction motivates all kinds of human behavior. Evolutionary psychologists David Buss and Lisa Dedden suggest that when faced with competition over a sexual partner, women tend to implement a set of very specific stratagems such as decreasing a rival's desirability or questioning her virtue. Just as Buss and Dedden could have predicted, Caroline attempts to shame Elizabeth in front of Georgiana.

"In the imprudence of anger," Caroline "took the first opportunity of saying, with sneering civility: 'Pray, Miss Eliza, are not the ——shire Militia removed from Meryton?'" She declares that the move must be a terrible loss to her family, implying (not quite untruthfully) that the Bennet girls are free with their attentions. Oblivious of Georgiana's past, Caroline renders herself even less popular when she asks after Wickham. "She had merely intended to discompose Elizabeth" and "make her betray a sensibility which might injure her in Darcy's opinion." Instead of reminding him of Lydia and Kitty's "follies and absurdities" with the military, Caroline threatens to reopen a Darcy family wound.

Unsuccessful, Caroline becomes erratic, "venting her feelings in criticisms on Elizabeth's person, behavior, and dress." Attempting to put Lizzie in her place as a bonneted bumpkin, Caroline announces that she has never seen someone as altered as Elizabeth, declaring her grown brown and coarse. Prattling on, Caroline admits that she had never seen any beauty in her, knowing damn well that Darcy had.

As if she were describing a prize horse at the county fair, Caroline points out a litany of Elizabeth's defects. Although she allows that her rival's teeth "are tolerable," Caroline finds that her eyes "have a sharp, shrewish look, which I do not like at all." Caroline's words have the opposite effect of what she intended in taunt after foolish taunt. Instead of drawing attention to Elizabeth's flaws, her judgments and comparisons only make her appear petty. When Georgiana fails to join in on her verbal tirade, she tries again with Darcy. "How very ill Miss Eliza Bennet looks this morning," she dangles.

Here, Austen teaches us an important lesson. Warning us that "angry people are not always wise," the narrator blithely notes that, "persuaded as Miss Bingley was that Darcy admired Elizabeth, this was not the best method of recommending herself." Caroline, seeing Darcy "at last look somewhat nettled," felt some sort of a triumph. Pressing him to speak, she continued, "I remember, when we first knew her in Hertfordshire, how amazed we all were to find that she was a reputed beauty." She reminisces on their shared understanding of the past. "I particularly recollect your saying one night," she cites, "she a beauty!—I should as soon call her mother a wit."

As much as I want to resent Caroline for her treatment of Elizabeth, I can't. Through Miss Bingley, Austen shows me aspects of myself, bringing past fears and jealousies to life. Caroline is everywhere, both in the Regency and today, reminding me that we are all struggling in some way. Lizzie and Caroline have much more in common than they would care to admit; the same was true of my difficult boss and me. Like our fictional counterparts, we struggled to determine our futures in incredibly patriarchal environments.

MAKE PEACE WITH THE CAROLINES IN YOUR WORLD

It would be easy for Caroline and Elizabeth to hate each other until the end of their days. Instead, Caroline's behavior teaches Elizabeth the genuine stakes at hand. Before her trip to Derbyshire, Pemberley was an unimaginable prize in a world where Mr. Collins could be considered a good catch.

Austen is unique in not dealing Caroline a dramatic comeuppance. Instead of relegating the character to a life of lonely poverty, Austen allows Miss Bingley to remain a part of the Pemberley set. Although she couldn't claim Darcy as her own, by "paying off every arrear of civility to Elizabeth," she became a welcome guest in their home, showing us that we have it in our power to repair relationships with other women if we really want to.

Isabella Thorpe

Smiles of Exquisite Misery

There is nothing I would not do for those who are really my
friends. I have no notion of loving people by halves; it is not my
nature. My attachments are always excessively strong.

—ISABELLA THORPE, *NORTHANGER ABBEY*

Deceptively charming, Isabella Thorpe's inspirational words on friendship separate the true Janeite from the amateur. Available for purchase
on mugs, magnets, T-shirts, and tote bags, the quote makes it easy to believe that Isabella is a kind-hearted, generous gal pal. Anyone who's read
Austen's gothic-influenced *Northanger Abbey* knows the truth; Isabella
Thorpe is a wolf disguised in muslin and lace. Bearing no resemblance
to real intimacy, her connections with the novel's gullible heroine are no
more than convenient tools to advance her social objectives.

For me, the satiric, coming-of-age narrative *Northanger Abbey* is
Austen's equivalent of a high school rom-com. Although published
after Austen's death, it was the first novel the author sold. Originally titled *Susan*, Austen began work on the story when she wasn't much older
than its wide-eyed main character. A London bookseller bought the
manuscript right after its completion in 1803 yet failed to do anything
with it. For years, Austen attempted to get it back to have its fate in her
own hands. Finally, in 1816, her brother Henry was able to re-purchase
it for the same price she had sold it for—a whopping ten pounds.

The narrative begins when we meet our (renamed) heroine, Catherine Moreland. She's introduced as being a perfectly average and unexceptional girl. She's a naive, reformed tomboy with little experience in the big, wide world and indeed no knowledge of the cliques and stratagems of other young women of her age group.

Catherine is brought to Bath to be a companion to her childless neighbors, the Allens. It's a familiar young-adult story trope referred to by screenwriter Robert McKee as "a stranger in a strange land." Catherine is Cady Heron, moving from homeschooling in Africa to the treacherous hallways of the American high school and learning their animalistic ways. She's Rory Gilmore, entering the halls of elite Chilton Academy. She's Hermione Granger, discovering an entirely new way of life at Hogwarts.

Catherine's first days in Bath are frustrating. Not knowing anyone except her chaperones, Catherine can't actively participate in public life—and public life is precisely what being in Bath during the season was all about. Winter in Bath wasn't only about taking the (disturbingly odiferous) health-giving waters. It was about a packed schedule of concerts, plays, and balls, all held in the beautiful assembly rooms in the heart of the city.

THINGS ARE MORE FUN IN PAIRS

Catherine's problem is solved when Mrs. Allen runs into an old schoolmate. Although the two ladies were never close and hadn't even thought of each other in decades, their bond is quickly renewed based on their mutual social needs. For her part, Mrs. Allen is delighted to find in Mrs. Thorpe a "good-humored, well-meaning woman" with several daughters to keep Catherine entertained. As a bonus, Mrs. Allen delights in the Thorpe family being less affluent than she is. Instead of the richness of children, Mrs. Allen is rich in fine dresses. The two former schoolmates spend their days in Bath talking *at* each other about the things they value most. Dialogue would be a generous term for their parallel monologues; one prattles about her children, the other about her expensive gowns. The message is clear: never underestimate the value of a good gossip and someone to be young with, regardless of your age.

Not only were the two older ladies perfectly contented, but their young charges also hit it off. Doe-eyed Catherine finds a friend in the eldest Thorpe daughter, Isabella. Regency propriety meant that young, unmarried women of their social class couldn't go out alone into public. Instead, they were reliant on each other to explore their world.

Contemporary research shows that not much has changed since Austen's day. Unseasoned girls often prefer to move in packs, whether to school dances or simply to the bathroom. It's not hard to imagine modern parallels to Catherine and Isabella's relationship; twenty-first-century girls still sit together at the same cafeteria table every day or spend their weekends texting endlessly to keep up on the latest gossip.

Isabellas and Catherines are everywhere. Each young woman offers something that the other doesn't have. Four years her elder, Isabella becomes Catherine's mentor in everything that was Bath: the shops, the books, the boys. For Catherine, Isabella represents freedom. Isabella revels in having an admiring acquaintance allowing her to separate herself from her younger sisters.

The eldest of three girls, Isabella is used to shepherding them. She's their role model. By "imitating her air, and dressing in the same style," the younger two girls "did very well." Naive Catherine is the perfect candidate for Isabella's coterie, and her naiveté and unfamiliarity with Bath allow the older girl to shine. The two become even more closely bound when they discover that Catherine's brother James had been a guest of the Thorpe family during university breaks. This loose association is enough to accelerate affection between them. Austen tells us that "the progress of the friendship between Catherine and Isabella was quick as its beginning had been warm." Like their chaperones, the pair become inseparable. Catherine was "soon invited to accept an arm of the eldest Miss Thorpe and take a turn with her about the room." Heady stuff indeed.

CHAPTER 2

IT PAYS TO BE SKEPTICAL OF FAST FRIENDSHIPS

Any girl who has moved to a new school or attended sleep-away camp by herself could have warned Catherine not to become too close to Isabella too quickly. That first, overly friendly girl in such situations isn't always the social savior one would hope for. Instead, she may be using you to become hers. This is undoubtedly the case with Isabella and Catherine as they bumble their way through Bath's obstacle-ridden marriage market.

The outer appearance of their attachment is charmingly old-fashioned. They "called each other by their Christian name" and "were always arm in arm when they walked, pinned up each other's train for the dance, and were not to be divided in the set." If the weather kept them inside, "they were still resolute in meeting in defiance of wet and dirt and shut themselves up, to read novels together."

Based on years of work with high school girls from various social backgrounds, parenting educator Rosalind Wiseman created a glossary of their conduct. Her bestselling guidebook, *Queen Bees and Wannabes: Helping Your Daughter Survive Cliques, Gossip, Boyfriends, and Other Realities of Adolescence*, is as disturbing as it is fascinating. In Wiseman's terms, Isabella is a Queen Bee: attractive, charismatic, and reliant on fear and control in her friendships. Isabella appears to be omnipotent, holding power over both boys and girls her age. Wiseman explains that younger women seek these bonds to "navigate the perils and insecurities of adolescence. There's a chain of command, and they operate as one in their interactions with their environment." Adults don't worry Queen Bees. They do their best to ingratiate themselves to teachers and parents, deflecting suspicion from their sketchy actions.

Queens like Isabella enjoy being the center of attention, strategically meting out affection while refusing to take responsibility for their deeds. According to Wiseman, Isabella's demonstrative affection for Catherine is typical of Queen Bee behavior. By making her feel special and unique, Isabella instills a sense of dependency and fierce loyalty in Catherine. Without her, Catherine would be back to trailing Mrs.

Allen and hoping for a seat at the assembly rooms rather than exploring social life in Bath. Girls like Catherine are most prone to the spells of a Queen when they start at a new school or are members of the youngest grade. Their presence upsets the current social hierarchy, and her peers will test where she fits in.

Isabella's true nature begins to show after their brothers arrive in town. Strolling through Bath stalking free-range bachelors, Isabella and Catherine happen upon John Thorpe and James Moreland. They continue their path as a foursome, with James and Isabella leading the way. Isabella is satisfied with the situation, although she doesn't lose sight of the young men they had been trailing. Austen sardonically relates that "so pure and uncoquettish were her feelings," that "Isabella was so far from seeking to attract their notice that she looked back at them only three times."

The message is clear: Isabella is a huntress.

WHEN PEOPLE SHOW YOU WHO THEY ARE, BELIEVE THEM

As soon as there is an eligible bachelor in the mix, Isabella's words and actions diverge. At first, her hypocrisy seems harmless. Knowing that the younger girl is dependent on her for outside entertainment, Isabella dictates the day's activities and makes Catherine wait for her attention. Instead of their former companionable walks and chats about the terrors of gothic novels, talk becomes all about the boys. Isabella transfers her primary focus to James, leaving Catherine questioning her affection.

Today's young women know this behavior all too well. Wiseman reveals that "in trying to please a boy," it's not unusual for a girl to "betray and sacrifice her friendships with girls." At this, I hang my head in shameful recognition. As a fourteen-year-old, having a boy call me on the phone was thrilling—so much so that my friend's crush on him completely escaped my hormone-intoxicated mind. As much as I hate to admit it, I, too, have foolishly traded real friends for pimply four-week flirtations.

Maybe because of this recognition, it's hard at first to blame Isabella for being wrapped up in her thoughts about James. Our understanding wanes as we experience her ignoring Catherine's desperation to talk about the boy she likes. Gossiping about boys is a normal part of adolescent female experience, and Wiseman advises that it is a crucial bonding mechanism. Girls ride a rollercoaster of feelings from around age twelve onward. From puppy love to obsession, the first thing that most girls do after speaking to a boy is call a girlfriend. Together, Wiseman relates, we "analyze every word of the conversation and discuss every nuance." Often, Wiseman tells us, girls spend more time talking to another girl *about* a boy than talking *to* the boy himself. This tendency is entirely understandable, considering how terrifying and unapproachable teenage boys can be to the average teenage girl.

Unlike Catherine, Isabella is older and more confident of herself and her charms, with less need to dissect every encounter with her beau. As soon as James shows up, their once steadfast friendship rapidly becomes perfunctory. Rendezvousing at a ball, Isabella goes through what the narrator calls "the usual ceremonial of meeting her friend." This includes "smiling and affectionate haste, of admiring the set of her gown and envying the curl of her hair." The two girls follow "their chaperones, arm in arm, into the ballroom, whispering to each other whenever a thought occurred, and supplying the place of many ideas by a squeeze of the hand or a smile of affection."

At first, all seems right in the world. Isabella promises that she wouldn't dream of dancing if Catherine couldn't join her. Her rigid stance lasts a whole three minutes before Isabella declares, "my dear creature, I am afraid I must leave you." Instead of admitting her infidelity, Isabella passive-aggressively blames James. "Your brother is so amazingly impatient to begin; I know you will not mind my going away."

YOU ARE OFTEN THE ONLY ADVOCATE FOR YOUR FEELINGS

Catherine very certainly *did* mind being left alone. Fortunately for Isabella, she "had too much good nature to make any opposition."

With a sense of drama known only to teenagers, Catherine felt "disgraced in the eye of the world." Being left alone without a friend or a dance partner, she regretted that no one else could know that "the misconduct of another" was "the true source of her debasement."

This sentiment certainly resonates. According to Wiseman, being seen alone, without a girlfriend, can be a daunting proposition. Not having a friend can feel like carrying a sign marked "I'm not worthy" in bold, red letters. Wiseman explains that friendship becomes as essential as air in adolescence, and its absence can feel like a drastic punishment. As a result, she warns parents, "girls may try to avoid being alone at all costs, including remaining in an abusive friendship."

Reading Catherine Morland, this seems to have been as accurate in the Regency as today. Fortunately for Jane Austen, her best friend was her sister, and she never had to fear being left alone. In contrast, Phyllis Chesler's work on indirect female aggression, *Woman's Inhumanity to Woman,* shows that "girls care more about being included than they do about whether they are ranked as dominant or subordinate." For many, Chesler claims, the most significant terror is "being excluded or rejected. When this happens, a girl experiences social aloneness in the universe." At least in youth, even the most introverted of us tend to be pack animals.

Often, Chesler finds, girls will suffer narcissistic, volatile friendships in silence. Some see developing a new companion as a struggle, and many girls report simply not having "the heart to begin anew." They worry that saying no to a peer could open her up to "pitiless exclusion."

Chesler finds that in the attempt to avoid harming any last, fragile threads of connection, many try their best not to disagree with or upset their friends. They withhold their true thoughts and feelings. Although it may not seem fair, fears of being cut off and abandoned are justified. After all, girls like Catherine rely on the Isabellas of the world to navigate the social scene.

With all that's at stake, it's no wonder Catherine doesn't dare criticize Isabella's terrible behavior. Deflecting blame, the older girl claims to have spent the evening "scolding" James to seek his sister "to such a degree, my dear Catherine, you would be quite amazed." What could Catherine say to such a statement?

Once again, Austen's Regency characters parallel Wiseman's twenty-first-century work. Despite the two-century time gap, Isabella's behavior remains typical of the age group. Then, as now, boyfriends are crucial for young women; not only do they increase a girl's self-esteem, but boyfriends also can advance their status among other girls. Having a boyfriend is considered evidence that a young woman fits in with societal expectations. Wiseman warns parents that, fair or not, teenage girls often "understand that their social status and identity are tied to relationships with boys." Pressure to fit in can be so great that even when they know better, a girl may ignore her once-dependable moral compass to please a boy.

This isn't a purely North American phenomenon. Evolutionary psychologist Joyce Benenson's work indicates that girls in Europe and Africa are just as willing to betray one another to bond with a boy. Injured girls take the abuse exceptionally seriously, and they report "greater anger, hurt, and jealousy than boys towards close same-sex friends, especially if they were abandoned for a romantic partner."

With this insight, it's not hard to see why contemporary readers can identify with Catherine Moreland. She's gentle-hearted, easily impressed, and kind of a dope. Despite her over-idolization of Henry Tilney, her over-dramatization of General Tilney, and her naive trust in her flawed friend, we feel protective of her. We watch in concern as her friendship with Isabella becomes increasingly lopsided. Separated by time, we can see the breadcrumbs of affection Isabella tosses to her to keep her love. Isabella's priority is James. The pair became so occupied with each other that Isabella only had time to bestow one smile, one squeeze of the hand, and one "dearest Catherine" to her obedient friend.

Although Isabella claimed to have thousands of things to say to Catherine, it is not to be; "it appeared as if they were never to be together again." At this point in the novel, Austen provides readers with delightfully dramatic oxymorons only possible in late puberty or community theater. Catherine was forced to witness both Isabella's "smiles of most exquisite misery" and "laughing eye of utter despondency." Poor Catherine was lost.

Rereading the story as an adult, I begin to feel a bit of concern for Catherine's ability to judge others at this point. It takes several repeats before she even *begins* "to doubt the happiness of a situation which, confining her entirely to her friend and brother, gave her very little share in the notice of either." Eventually, Isabella has so little time for Catherine that she "could not avoid a little suspicion" that her friend didn't have her best interests at heart. Harsh words, indeed.

Things get darker when Isabella and her buffoon brother John insist that Catherine chaperone an impromptu excursion in their carriage. Catherine demurs, citing a previous engagement. At her refusal, Isabella escalates from politely inviting the girl to manipulative lies. Finally, Catherine could *almost* suspect Isabella of not having her best interests at heart. Instead, Isabella commands Catherine to forget her plans and not "be so dull, my dearest creature."

IF SOMEONE PRESSURES YOU INTO CONTACT WITH SOMEONE YOU DREAD, RUN

According to Wiseman, Catherine's reluctance to deny Isabella is entirely usual. Her work with hundreds of female bullying survivors showed that young women are often unable to deal with conflict. Instead, they avoid it at all costs, ending up in some sketchy situations as a result. Like Catherine, they find it difficult to trust their instincts, leading them to doubt what they saw or experienced. Through interviews, Wiseman discovered that girls learn to internalize their feelings to avoid confrontation at an early age. By channeling their feelings of hurt and anger, incidents are brushed off but not forgotten. Instead, girls "store away unresolved conflicts with the precision of a bookkeeper, building a stockpile that increasingly crowds her emotional landscape and social choices."

Isabella relies on Catherine's silence. Typical of what Wiseman refers to as "Queen Bee" behavior, Isabella holds purposeful control over the terms of their relationships. For Wiseman, this is "a signal aspect of relational aggression." Readers witness Catherine's increasing anxiety when conversing with Isabella, "looking down as she spoke," and being "fearful of Isabella's smile." With these descriptions, Austen anticipates what Wiseman refers to as "Sidekick" demeanor. In Wiseman's terms, Sidekicks look to the Queen for advice and let her manipulate their actions.

The Sidekick role has both negative and positive connotations for contemporary young women. Wiseman cautions parents that teenage Sidekicks often lose their own identities. Being close to a Queen offers them a sense of power and popularity, which they would unlikely experience on their own. Reassuringly for parents, such positions aren't permanent. Wiseman predicts that if separated from the Queen, a Sidekick "can alter her behavior for the better." In contrast, "a Queen Bee is more likely to find another Sidekick and begin again."

Catherine *does* try to disentangle herself from Isabella on several occasions. Isabella and John always need an extra girl to round out their everlasting carriage rides into the Bath countryside. They certainly don't make it easy for Catherine to refuse. The older girl responds to Catherine's resistance with honeyed tones, "calling on her in the most affectionate manner, addressing her by the most endearing names." After weeks of neglect, Catherine is once again Isabella's "dearest, sweetest Catherine." Isabella feigns disbelief that her sweet-tempered friend could refuse such an innocent request from "a friend who loved her so dearly."

Failing to convince Catherine, Isabella tries a different approach. Attempting to guilt her into acquiescence, Isabella reproaches her for having more affection for Miss Tilney "than for her best and oldest friends." At this, middle-aged me nostalgically aches for the time calculations of teenagers. Isabella has only known Catherine a few days longer than she has the Tilneys, a youthful eternity.

Finding the Tilneys standing in her way of an outdoor adventure, Isabella encourages Catherine to malign them. She badgers Catherine about her visit to their lodgings, calling the family haughty and proud. Again, the hyperbolic timekeeping of the young rears its head. Isabella "had long suspected the family to be very high, and this made it certain. Such insolence of behavior as Miss Tilney's she had never heard of in her life!" When Catherine attempts to correct her, Isabella declares, "Oh! Don't defend her!"

GOSSIP IS CURRENCY

Wiseman finds that 99.99 percent of girls gossip. Although it may sometimes bear the outward appearance of idle chatter, tittle-tattle at any age is a tool to bolster feelings of self-esteem, social competency, and alliances with others. Isabella's disparagement of the Tilneys is a marked attempt to solidify her relationship with Catherine in Wiseman's terms.

It doesn't work.

A sense of reluctance toward Isabella becomes a repeated theme as the narrative progresses. Catherine is shown "resolutely turning away her eyes," avoiding eye contact with Isabella and the rest of her family. Isabella's narcissistic nature echoes again and again. We learn that while Catherine "could not tell a falsehood even to please Isabella," it does not even matter. She "was spared her friend's dissenting voice" by not even waiting for Catherine to answer her; "her own feelings entirely engrossed her."

At this point, Austen equates the relationship between the two young women with warfare. Although Catherine's arm is still linked within Isabella's, the narrator tells us that their hearts are at war. Catherine is in emotional chaos, as "one moment she was softened, at another irritated; always distressed, but always steady."

Like so many, I can only be thankful that we only go through high school once in our lives. For anyone just a little outside of the norm, the daily dodging of insidious comments can be both confusing and exhausting. It's no wonder that things tend to get better in our mid-twenties when our pre-frontal cortex is finally fully developed, and we can take a metaphorical step back and gain perspective.

While teenage quibbles may appear harmless at first, they take a darker turn when Isabella tries to coerce Catherine into a relationship with her savage brother. It's essential to be precise. *At no point in the story* has Catherine expressed any interest in the man. She has been polite to him over the weeks. Not because she likes him, but because he is the brother of a good friend, and she has been brought up to do so.

Despite her pointed apathy to the lout, Isabella attempts to gaslight Catherine into marriage when he declares that it is expected. Isabella accuses her "sweetest Catherine" of being absurd and dishonest; after all, his attentions were so evident that even "a child must have noticed." All it took was for him to write a letter to his family, informing them that he expected a positive response to his proposal. With a man's words, Catherine's fate was considered sealed. As a man, John's words aren't questioned. She must be wrong; Isabella declares that she gave him positive encouragement. After all, "he says so in his letter."

Wiseman claims that young women like Isabella enjoy matchmaking. In setting up another girl, she becomes more closely bound to her, beholden for her status as part of a pair. The threat to Catherine to form an alliance with John Thorpe is real, and Isabella feigns indignation at her denial. "I do not pretend to determine what your thoughts and designs in time past may have been," she insinuates, claiming that her friend knowingly flirted with John, encouraging him more than Catherine was willing to admit. Essentially, Isabella calls her friend a wishy-washy tease, meaning one thing today and another tomorrow.

The hairs on the back of my neck rise when Catherine's protests fall on deaf ears.

Maybe I'm too sensitive. Perhaps I have known too many girls pressured into relationships to keep their friends happy. It's these words, this move from Isabella, that shocks me the most, and for good reason. According to the US Department of Health and Human Services, it's not only the John Thorpes of the world who coerce women into believing that they owe a guy physical attention. It's women as well. Often, it starts "innocently" when Grandma pressures her little sunshine to "kiss Uncle Kevin goodbye" or "sit on Grandpa's lap," although it feels creepy. These girls learn quickly that their bodies don't belong only to them; they are meant to please others.

Fortunately, the actual consequences of coercion in a novel are nil. At worst, Austen's fictional scenario could result in an unhappy fictitious marriage.

It's in real homes and workplaces where actual harm happens, causing irreparable physical and emotional damage. If recent events have taught us anything, it's that some parts of our society will never believe the word of women. They will never acknowledge the pain behind #MeToo. For some women and men, pussies will always be there for the grabbing. As long as brave women who dare tell of their ordeals face death threats, slander, and mockery for being a victim, this will sadly remain true.

Isabella's strong-arm tactics certainly make it easier for me to let go of her as a friend. She's a traitor to Catherine (and womankind), trying to gaslight her social protégé into an unhappy marriage. She betrays her fiancé as well, behaving erratically as soon as James Morland leaves town. Despite their engagement, Isabella flirts openly with another man. Even at this, gullible Sidekick Catherine is reluctant to suspect her friend. However, she "could not help watching her closely" when they were alone. Isabella, it seems, was suddenly "an altered creature."

Unsurprisingly, Wiseman warns that "girls can be each other's worst enemies." Intense friendships between young women can often be "confusing, frustrating, and humiliating." The joy and security of having a best friend are shattered by breakups and betrayals for many. Wiseman cautions parents not to play down these experiences, as the emotional response to the ups and downs of friendship can be just as intense as those in intimate, adult relationships.

Cute bonnets can hide a horrific set of horns.

Like many, Catherine keeps the peace by remaining silent. Still, she can't entirely turn a blind eye to her friend's behavior in public. "What could be meant by such unsteady conduct, what her friend could be at, was beyond her comprehension," we learn. "Isabella could not be aware of the pain she was inflicting," the generous girl muses. "But it was a degree of wilful thoughtlessness which Catherine could not but resent." It comes as a relief when our heroine is invited to spend time with her friends, the Tilneys, at their romantic, gothic-sounding home, Northanger Abbey.

In relationships, there are two schools of thought. For some, absence makes the heart grow fonder. For others, out of sight means out of mind. Isabella belongs to the latter. Not only is she perfectly capable of banishing James from her thoughts, but she also blocks Catherine from her mind as soon as the girl leaves Bath.

After such intense, ardent proclamations of love and affection, of deep and committed friendship, we can't blame Catherine for believing that Isabella would keep in contact. Instead, she is dropped altogether. Away at Northanger, Catherine becomes confused, growing more nervous by Isabella's silence by the day. "She was quite impatient to know how the Bath world went on and how the rooms were attended," we learn. Who can forget the teenage need to know about everyone and everything? Catherine relied upon Isabella for this information, somehow still believing that they were friends. She even tells the Tilneys that "Isabella had promised and promised again; and when she promised a thing, she was so scrupulous in performing it!"—*not*.

Being dropped by a friend or close colleague can sting. I hate to admit how many times I had to excuse myself to the ladies' room for a quiet weep at my very first corporate job. Financially self-reliant for the first time in my life and living in a foreign country, the stakes were incredibly high. There was a pool of us, all in our late twenties, working as assistants to middle-aged white guys. Being kept out of the loop for a meeting or event, not cc'd on an email, meant that a colleague couldn't do her job correctly. Being pointedly not included in the informal roster of assistant lunch dates could result in a woman missing out on meaningful information. Although the stakes must have seemed ridiculously low from the outside, these slights made many of us fear for our jobs.

Would I have expected the same from a male colleague? I highly doubt it.

In their study on intra-gender micro-violence between professional women, professors Sharon Mavin, Gina Grandy, and Jannine Williams found that participants "commented upon the severity of their emotional experience" when it came at the hands of other women. In 2023, society continues to expect that women treat each other as sisters. Like me, Mavin, Grandy, and Williams reported being personally challenged by research on the subject, because intra-gender aggression is so painful and close to heart.

As Mavin and her colleagues may have predicted, Catherine has no trouble seeing through John Thorpe's coarse stratagems; she does not need him. It takes her much longer to see through Isabella's false claims of love for her brother and herself. Austen describes Catherine's slow puzzlement as she tries to tune out the many "contradictions in her friend's statements and actions." Ever hopeful, Catherine expects far more from her female friend than she would a man.

Catherine counts on Isabella, both as a friend and a future sister-in-law, and Isabella betrays this trust as soon as she senses a better offer. Hoping for an attachment to the Northanger heir, Captain Frederick Tilney, Isabella breaks off her engagement with James and abandons Catherine altogether. Only when the hope of this second match fizzles out does she attempt to reinstate intimacy with the Morlands.

In typical Queen Bee fashion, Isabella takes no responsibility for wounding both Catherine and James. Conveniently forgetting the fact that it was she who called off their engagement, Isabella claims to be "fearful of some misunderstanding." She hopes that Catherine's "kind offices will set all right." She unconvincingly pleads that "he is the only man I ever did or could love, and I trust you will convince him of it."

At this, readers learn that "such a strain of shallow artifice could not impose even upon Catherine. Its inconsistencies, contradictions, and falsehood struck her from the very first." Finally, Catherine was ashamed of her friendship with Isabella and having loved her; she saw that her professions of attachment were as empty as her excuses.

For English professor Beth Lau, Catherine's eventual understanding of Isabella's true nature reflects her psychological development. Describing "Catherine's Education in Mindreading," in *Jane Austen and Sciences of the Mind,* Lau shows how our heroine slowly develops a more sophisticated Theory of Mind (ToM). In basic terms, ToM is the ability to reason about what others are thinking and feeling. It is a critical socio-cognitive skill that develops throughout childhood. Citing psychologists Simon Baron-Cohen, John Tooby, and Leda Cosmides, Lau claims that Austen highlights the need for a "fully functioning Theory of Mind mechanism." Without it, a young woman can't navigate her entrance into the social world.

According to Lau, Catherine's initial inability to identify Isabella's manipulative motives leaves her open to exploitation by the older girl. Lau underpins Catherine's learning curve in evolutionary terms, proposing that (like me) Catherine turns to literature for essential life lessons. Of course, part of what bonded Catherine to Isabella in the first place was their shared love of gothic novels. Lau reports that what Austen described instinctively two centuries ago is now gaining "support from contemporary neuroscience and evolutionary psychology, which have begun to explore the cognitive and adaptive functions of literature."

STEP AWAY FROM FALSE FRIENDS

In the end, readers rejoice at Catherine's realization of Isabella's true nature. At last, she stops being a pawn in Isabella's matchmaking game. She sees through Isabella's sudden resumption of correspondence. "Write to James on her behalf! No, James should never hear Isabella's name mentioned by her again." Catherine is hurt. "She must think me an idiot," she cries, "or she could not have written so." Catherine understands what Isabella has been at, declaring her "a vain coquette." Sadly, she realizes that the scheming hussy had never had a genuine regard for her or her brother. She dramatically declares that she wished she "had never known her."

Isabella fulfills a vital role in *Northanger Abbey*, offering readers insight into the dangers of an overly trusting nature. Literature scholar Susan Ostrov Weisser refers to mean girl characters like Isabella as "wonderful-terrible bitch figures," who serve as warnings. To get the man they want, false friends will do anything they need and pretend to be anything they need to be to make it happen. For Weisser, types like Isabella are "fluid in identity" and outrageous in behavior.

Whether referring to Weisser, Wiseman, Lau, or Simmons, it seems that we will never entirely escape the false friendships that Austen built into her narratives. Her descriptions of the joys and the agonies of female relationships remain fresh simply because they are accurate. Just because we have high expectations of our female peers, real friendship isn't simply a given.

Of course, Austen offers readers more than just mean girls. The author herself knew the joy that stems from true friendship. Together, Catherine and Eleanor Tilney enjoy the happiest of endings. Each demonstrates a generosity of spirit unknown to the Isabella Thorpes of the world; neither boasts of their "excessively strong" attachment to each other, they simply show them. For all of her "suffering" and "unpretending merit," Eleanor is rewarded with the man and the home of her choice. Like the real friend she is, she immediately uses her influence as "Your Ladyship" to undo the harms the Thorpe siblings instigated.

With Eleanor's help, readers can close the book, satisfied with the knowledge that "bells rang and everybody smiled" as our beloved "Henry and Catherine were married."

CHAPTER 3

Monstrous Pretty Lucy Steele

Keep your friends close, your enemies even closer.
—SUN TZU

Of all the loathsome, villainous female characters Austen brings to life, *Sense and Sensibility* includes the very worst. Readers are on high alert from the first moment Fanny Dashwood and Lucy Steele slither onto the scene; things are going to get ugly. While our heroine, Elinor Dashwood, is making sensibly mature decisions about what is best for her mother and sisters, Fanny and Lucy are out for blood—Fanny for her family and Lucy for herself. As a wealthy wife and mother, Fanny can afford to be openly hostile to other women. Unmarried, uneducated, and poor, Lucy takes a stealthy approach, pursuing her target with small but deadly steps.

Ever the opportunist, Lucy sashays between ingratiating and backstabbing, marking her territory with words and objects. Although the term hadn't existed in Austen's day, Lucy Steele is the epitome of the modern term *frenemy*. First added to the *Oxford English Dictionary* in 2008, the ancient admonition "keep your friends close, your enemies even closer" demonstrates the sentiment's longevity. Hardly a woman alive hasn't experienced the smile and sting of a false friend.

CHAPTER 3

ALLIANCES BETWEEN WOMEN ARE
NOT ALWAYS AS THEY SEEM

Sense and Sensibility begins with the three Dashwood girls and their mother being driven out of their family home. Following the death of their father, they are begrudgingly tolerated in what is now their half-brother's house. Things become uncomfortable when the eldest, Elinor, develops feelings for her sister-in-law's brother, Edward Ferrars.

Both Edward's mother and sister are determined to make an advantageous match for him. A union with the almost penniless Elinor is objectionable, and her welcome in her old home quickly wears out. Fortunately for the Dashwood ladies, they escape the ire of Edward's relations by retreating to a cottage owned by their relative, Sir John Middleton. The move is a sharp degradation, from a stately family home to a pokey rental. Nevertheless, they take pleasure in its distance from their mercenary sister-in-law.

Their country peace is short-lived. Sir John proves to be a chatty, sociable man who shares his home with his wife and her mother, whose joy in life is matchmaking. Sir John insists that the Dashwoods meet and entertain every houseguest the Middletons may have, and they have many. Immediately, the ladies receive so many invitations to private balls, water parties, dinners, and teas that they begin to reevaluate the actual cost of their modest rent. Although dull, the events themselves are harmless.

That is, until Lucy and Anne Steele arrive to stay.

Oddly, neither the Dashwoods nor the Middletons know the girls. Ever-jovial Sir John and his mother-in-law met the two by happenstance on a trip to Exeter. After a brief chat, they discover themselves to be distantly related and immediately invite them to visit. As if this reasoning wasn't flimsy enough, Sir John declares to Elinor and Marianne that the Steeles know them.

Sir John triumphantly announces that the unfamiliar ladies long to make their acquaintance; the Steeles have heard that the Dashwoods are the loveliest creatures in the world. Just how and where they got this information is of no interest to Sir John. For him, the pair represents fresh blood for family parties, and his thirst for novelty means that he'll take the girls precisely as they come. As "Lucy is monstrous pretty," what harm could there be?

WATCH THEIR EYES

The initial meeting between the Dashwoods and Steeles brings no enlightenment. Although Anne proves to be a dolt, her sister Lucy turns out to be an attractive young woman with "a sharp, quick eye." Elinor and Marianne find her disappointing despite displaying "a smartness of air." She simply has no natural "elegance or grace." One meeting was enough.

The same isn't true for the Steeles. They declare the Dashwood ladies to be "the most beautiful, elegant, accomplished, and agreeable girls they had ever beheld, and with whom they were particularly anxious to be better acquainted." Their companionship was inevitable. After all, rural Regency England wasn't known for its nonstop social scene. To make matters worse, "Sir John was entirely on the side of the Miss Steeles." Their good-natured landlord encouraged a "kind of intimacy" between the young women, which consisted of "sitting an hour or two together in the same room almost every day."

What a delight.

At yet another superfluous gathering, Elinor notices that what the newcomer lacks in cultivation, she makes up for in manipulation. Lucy knows her duty as a guest, doling out extravagant compliments toward Sir John and his family. Through their constant smiles, the Steele girls appear immune to the horrors of the Middleton brats. They play willing victims to a continuous barrage of undone sashes, hair-pulling, and petty theft. Instead of scolding them, Lucy and Anne establish themselves in Lady Middleton's heart by appearing "in continual raptures, extolling their beauty, courting their notice, and humoring their whims."

BEWARE OF SUCK-UPS

Elinor recognizes the usefulness of this behavior. It hasn't changed much over the centuries. Parents tend to thrive on praise for their children. I can attest that anyone who admires my (brilliant and handsome) only son earns a soft spot in my heart. Austen knows this as well. Describing the scene, she declares "a fond mother" to be "the most rapacious of human beings." Austen had clearly witnessed mothers in her social circle devouring compliments of their kids, from their height and weight to the rapidity of their potty training. While childless Austen herself never experienced that instinctive, visceral transformation from suburban soccer mom to blindly frenzied mama bear if anyone dared diss her offspring, she'd seen it happen in others.

Literature professor Lynda Hall points this out as well. In her work *Women and Value in Jane Austen's Novels*, Hall demonstrates how Lucy uses these mechanisms. Hall refers to her as "a woman who is driven by her inadequate expressed value to manipulate the social codes—using flattery to get her way." Lucy uses compliments to prime the Middletons into thinking well of her. Even though her flowery language leaves an aftertaste, I doubt many of us haven't done the same. True honesty can be a luxury; at job interviews and performance reviews, working women know that to speak out of turn can have costly consequences.

In contrast, Elinor and Marianne demonstrate a level of verbal integrity that the Steele girls simply cannot afford. Subtlety can be expensive. The Dashwoods remain on moral high ground, although Marianne's brutal truthfulness in word and deed could be interpreted as a refusal to cooperate in the expected social niceties. The Steeles are in a much weaker economic position than the Dashwoods. Unable to afford Marianne's principled rudeness, they're forced to simper and smile, admiring their betters to advance in the world. After flattering the Middletons, Lucy sets her sights on Elinor. She misses "no opportunity of engaging her in conversation," to strive "to improve their acquaintance," attempting to camouflage her fawning with "easy and frank communication of her sentiments."

In *Odd Girl Out: The Hidden Culture of Aggression in Girls*, educator Rachel Simmons describes this behavior as "alliance-building." This peer affirmation technique creates an "unspoken contract" between two young women. For young women like Lucy Steele, Simmons reports, "friendship is a weapon."

At first, Elinor thinks that Lucy is just bored. There isn't much to do at the Middletons, and Marianne refuses to engage with the Steeles at all. High-minded and sensitive, Marianne declares that she simply will not tolerate "anything like impertinence, vulgarity, inferiority of parts, or even difference of taste from herself." Since Elinor is more conventionally polite, she gets stuck keeping company with the Steeles. Beyond common interests, women are expected to be likable. As Simmons explains, "the sugar-and-spice image is powerful, and girls know it." She advises that an essential part of covert aggression "is looking like you would never mistreat someone in the first place."

BEING GOOD SOMETIMES HURTS

Like so many of us, Elinor is socialized to assume the role of "good girl" or caretaker. As Simmons explains, Western culture teaches young women that "they will be valued for their relationships with others," and "sensible" Elinor appears willing to accommodate. In contrast, "sensitive" Marianne doesn't feel compelled to conform. She is "at this time particularly ill-disposed, from the state of her spirits, to be pleased with the Miss Steeles or to encourage their advances." This leads Marianne to behave with "invariable coldness" toward them.

Even proper Elinor can't take the Steeles for very long. Although "Lucy was naturally clever," and "often just and amusing," Elinor could only stand her for half an hour—no more. They had nothing in common except their youth. Despite being the nieces of a teacher, Lucy and Anne are uneducated, ignorant, and illiterate—damning words for Austen's devoted readers. Even worse, Lucy wasn't even interested in improving herself. Elinor spotted her "want of information in the most common particulars" straight off. Lucy constantly makes basic linguistic errors, to the horror of the grammar police among us. She doesn't seem to understand the words she chooses. Lucy lacks "delicacy . . . rectitude, and integrity of mind, which her attentions, her assiduities, her flatteries at the Park betrayed."

It takes Elinor a bit longer than Marianne to reach the point of no return. In the end, even our patient heroine determines that she just can't bear friendship with "a person who joined insincerity with ignorance," and "whose want of instruction prevented their meeting in conversation on terms of equality." Lucy's sycophantic behavior toward the Middletons renders anything that was coming from her mouth "perfectly valueless."

And yet, despite her rejection by the Dashwood girls, Lucy refuses to let go. She's dead set on continuing contact with Elinor. Without connecting with Miss Dashwood, Lucy couldn't achieve the true objective of her visit to the Middletons—getting Elinor to back off from her man. After all, as Simmons points out, "the lifeblood of relational aggression is relationship."

Readers witness Lucy sidling up to Elinor at every opportunity. It's hard not to imagine her eyelashes fluttering in mock innocence as she slyly queries Elinor. "You will think my question an odd one, I dare say," Lucy purrs, "but pray, are you personally acquainted with your sister-in-law's mother, Mrs. Ferrars?"

Of course, Elinor thought the question was weird. Why on earth should this random, uncultured girl want to talk about such an arbitrary subject, stuck out in the godforsaken countryside so far from any of the Ferrars family? With her bewilderment clearly showing, Elinor answers that she had never met the woman in question.

Readers know what's up.

After all, we see Lucy in our mind's eye, attentively assessing Elinor as she gently sharpens her weapons. "Perhaps there may be reasons," Lucy intones, professing guilelessness by claiming, "I hope you will do me the justice of believing that I do not mean to be impertinent." Saddling up her Trojan horse, Lucy hesitantly ventures, "I cannot bear to have you think me impertinently curious. I am sure I would rather do anything in the world than be thought so by a person whose good opinion is so well worth having as yours." Bizarrely, the girl continues, "I should not have the smallest fear of trusting you."

Like many hidden aggressors, Lucy sticks with her weapon of choice: flattery. She suggests that "in such an uncomfortable situation as I am," Elinor's advice would be precious. There isn't much that pro-social Elinor can do but to reassure Lucy, offering her help. "If it could be of any use," Elinor admits. She admits that she had no idea that Lucy was at all connected with the Ferrars, confessing surprise "at so serious an inquiry into her character."

Austen describes Lucy's eyes as she speaks, cueing readers to the verbal bombshell she is about to drop. Looking down, she attempts to appear "amiably bashful, with only one side glance at her companion to observe its effect." Cunning Lucy admits, "Mrs. Ferrars is certainly nothing to me at present," but in time they should be very intimately connected, indeed.

Wink, wink, nudge, nudge.

Lucy's eyes serve as warning guideposts throughout the novel. By drawing her readers' attention to the character's "quick, sharp eye," readers instantly understand Lucy's deceptive nature. The same is true in modern life. Through her work with young women in American schools, Simmons shows that the behavior is well understood. "Girls, ever respectful, tend to aggress quietly," Simmons explains. "They flash looks, pass notes, and spread rumors. Their actions, though sometimes physical, are typically more psychological and thus invisible." Even the most observant outsider, Simmons relates, can fail to catch how these girls use their eyes to communicate, catching, narrowing, and withdrawing eye contact. For Simmons, such "nonverbal gesturing . . . is a hallmark of relational aggression." Although "infuriatingly empty of detail," it remains "bluntly clear."

Lucy's subversive ploy misses its object. Elinor has not recognized the truth. "Good heavens!" she demands, asking Lucy if she is engaged to Edward's younger brother, Robert. Feigning sheepishness, Lucy announces that no, Edward is her beau, through downcast eyes. "You may well be surprised," Lucy furtively murmurs. "It was always meant to be a great secret."

Lucy justifies disclosing this ghastly fact to an almost complete stranger by insinuating, "I never should have mentioned it to you, if I had not felt the greatest dependence in the world upon your secrecy." As for Elinor, she "turned towards Lucy in silent amazement, unable to divine the reason or object of such a declaration." Luckily, "she stood firm in incredulity and felt in no danger of a hysterical fit or a swoon." She, like us, is astonished, overcome with disbelief.

THE PRESSURE IS REAL

Gossip and aggression expert Frank McAndrew tells us that one of the biggest evils a young woman can commit is stealing—or being perceived to steal—a peer's boyfriend. McAndrew warns that romantic competition can have deadly consequences in today's world. In a 2018 *Psychology Today* article, he details the deaths by suicide of girls as young as age ten, motivated by relentless bullying by schoolmates accusing them of the crime.

It's impossible to know what Lucy Steele would have done if Regency England had had social media. Limited by the analog world, Lucy tries to block Elinor's interest in Edward the old-fashioned way, with subtle, indirect aggression. Couching her spite in terms of praise, Lucy tells her victim that even though no one else in the entire world knows about the engagement apart from her sister Anne, telling Elinor somehow made sense.

Nonsense.

Lucy carries a warning in her following words, announcing that she will tell Edward their shared confidence. Lucy simply cannot think that her beloved Mr. Ferrars "can be displeased when he knows I have trusted you because I know he has the highest opinion in the world of all your family." As if this wasn't enough, she pushes Elinor deep into the friend zone by declaring that her fiancé "looks upon yourself and the other Miss Dashwoods quite as his own sisters."

Sisterly love. How flattering.

Showing more composure than I had ever achieved when it came to a boy, Elinor remains silent. Elinor conceals her hurt where her sister Marianne would have been a howling basket case. Sensing resistance, Lucy liberally pours additional salt into the wound.

Of course, Lucy was not to blame.

No, the engagement was purely Edward's idea.

"Though you do not know him so well as me, Miss Dashwood," Lucy suggests, "you must have seen enough of him to be sensible he is very capable of making a woman sincerely attached to him." Lucy seems compelled to add physical evidence to her claim. Taking a miniature out of her pocket, she asks Elinor to "be so good as to look at this face. It does not do him justice, to be sure, but yet I think you cannot be deceived as to the person it was drew for."

Yes, she said "drew for."

One by one, Lucy adds additional layers of proof of her previous, unceded, rightful claim on Edward. A letter in his hand, him wearing a ring with a lock of her hair. Perhaps Elinor had seen it on him, Lucy inquires.

Of course, Elinor had seen it. She had even daydreamed that the hair was her own, clandestinely stolen so that he could have a piece of her always near him—what a tremendous letdown.

Dramatically describing the trials of her secret engagement, Lucy carefully produces a handkerchief as if to wipe away her mournful tears. In delightful understatement, Austen relates, "Elinor did not feel very compassionate." Lucy's pointed questions don't make things better. "What would you advise me to do in such a case, Miss Dashwood?" She pleads, "what would you do yourself?"

We readers know that Lucy poses the same question to Elinor that Elinor has already asked herself. Was it possible to remain close to Edward when his family was against it? Again, demonstrating a maturity I have never known, Elinor recuses herself from providing any "advice under such circumstances," telling Lucy that her judgment must be her guide.

The scene is a complex web of mind reading and attributions, with each character—and us, their audience—reading between the lines. Elinor had "little difficulty in understanding . . . her rival's intentions," believing Lucy to "be disposed to be jealous of her." For Elinor, "it was plain that Edward had always spoken highly in her praise, not merely from Lucy's assertion, but from her venturing to trust her on so short a personal acquaintance, with a secret so confessedly and evidently important."

WE KNOW THEY KNOW WE KNOW

Cognitive narratologists like University of Kentucky professor Lisa Zunshine explore passages like these to demonstrate Austen's uncanny ability to characterize complex mental states and our skill in following them. We know that Elinor's feelings for Edward are anything but platonic. We know that Elinor knows that Lucy is aware of her attachment to Edward and Edward's interest in Elinor. We (as well as Elinor and Lucy) know that Lucy intends to wound Elinor with her words, despite being cloaked in compliments. A modern comparison Zunshine offers is the *Friends* episode in which Rachel, Phoebe, and Joey know that Monica and Chandler know that they know about their secret relationship. These fascinating mind-reading exercises, Zunshine claims, are why humans love reading fiction.

It's not a surprise that women can relate to these experiences. After all, it's a part of our everyday lives. Developmental psychologists claim that as early as six years old, we begin to interpret the words and actions of others. Why is she invited to her house to play and not me? Why is that girl chosen first for sports teams and not me? What did she mean when she pretended not to see me at the mall? Why hasn't she reacted to my Insta post?

These types of disappointment aren't the most serious of crimes for many adolescents. Underscoring McAndrew's observations, sociologists Anne Campbell and Paula Stockley find that a dishearteningly high percentage of disagreements amongst young women are "centered—directly or indirectly—on men." In their work, Stockley and Campbell identify indirect aggression like Lucy's as a useful tool, "a successful strategy in delaying or removing rivals from the mating arena." If all goes well for Lucy, her carefully constructed conversation with Elinor will be enough to drive the other girl off. Understandably, Stockley and Campbell report that their findings are very unpopular within the feminist community, as they sadly deviate from ideological preferences.

Lucy's ostensibly innocent remarks put strong, upright Elinor in a pickle. She knows that Edward loves her, for "what other reason for the disclosure of the affair could there be, but that Elinor might be informed by it of Lucy's superior claims on Edward, and be taught to avoid him in [the] future?"

Lucy's tactics aren't unusual outside of fiction, but they can often backfire. Rosalind Wiseman contends that approaches like Lucy's often distort conflicts between young women. By initially attempting to build an alliance with Elinor, Lucy makes the situation last much longer than it would have if "played out directly." A more effective and common form of torment in today's world is for girls like Lucy to spread malicious gossip about their competitors. Damage to a young woman's social network can crush her spirit.

BE WARY OF SECRETS

At a loss, Elinor reminds Lucy that she never wanted to be her confidante. While assuring her that her secret was safe, she adds, "pardon me if I express some surprise at so unnecessary a communication. You must at least have felt that my being acquainted with it could not add to its safety." As Zunshine points out, readers begin attributing intentions to a character as soon as they act. Through past chapters, we already know that Elinor is better at adulting than her sister. We're sure that Lucy Steele can't be anything more than a scheming bitch. Why else would she have sucked up so extravagantly to the Middletons?

We can't help but be suspicious when Lucy simply smiles when Elinor challenges her. "Our first care has been to keep the matter secret," she murmurs. "You knew nothing of me or my family, and, therefore, there could be no occasion for ever mentioning my name to you." From that moment onward, Edward becomes the sole subject of their conversations. There was no way that Lucy would let Elinor forget that Edward was "hers." At that period in history, secret or not, a betrothal was legally binding. Only the female half of the equation could call things off. Her family could have rightly sued for damages if Edward had cast Lucy aside.

"Her little sharp eyes full of meaning," Lucy accuses Elinor of having a "coldness and displeasure," which made her feel uncomfortable. "I felt sure that you was angry with me" (yes, another Lucyism). A master of passive aggression, Lucy repeats her warning to Elinor. "If you knew what a consolation it was to me to relieve my heart speaking to you of what I am always thinking of every moment of my life, your compassion would make you overlook everything else, I am sure."

As if this wasn't enough, Lucy demands Elinor soothe her poor grieving heart. Ever careful, Elinor does as Simmons would predict; she protects herself by remaining silent. Simmons explains that silence "is deeply woven in the fabric of the female experience." For Simmons, girls' alliance-building represents "a rare intersection of peer approval with aggression."

In "'The Sword of a Woman': Gossip and Female Aggression," social psychologist Francis T. McAndrew's meta-analysis of communication like Lucy's shows that it's a valuable means to pass on negative information and detect betrayal. Lucy's cautious conversations provide her with critical insight into Elinor, whose behavior threatens to impact her future. McAndrew finds that instigators like Lucy are inevitably seeking damaging information despite using affiliative language. Anything positive "tends to be uninteresting."

Framing her message in terms of confidence at the same time as sending a warning to back off, Lucy confides, "I am rather of a jealous temper." Had she experienced the slightest change in Edward's behavior, "or any lowness of spirits that I could not account for, or if he had talked more of one lady than another," Lucy threatens, she would have "found out the truth in an instant."

And there it was, the clear and blatant truth behind the Steeles' sudden appearance at the Middletons.

LOOK FOR THE SOURCE

I'd love to think that Elinor's ability to keep her secret drives Lucy to distraction. If I had such a fantastic nugget of information, I'd want to spread it far and wide. I'd tweet a teardown of Lucy's inability to speak proper English and show a backbone in front of the Middleton children. I'd probably challenge Edward on Facebook, demanding to know how he could have allied himself to such a twit. Imagine a Regency *Jerry Springer Show*, if you will. From my experience in Facebook jail, such confrontations lead precisely to what Lucy wants. Edward would be shamed, his relationship with Elinor ruined, and all hope of their continued contact destroyed.

A more carefully considered reaction would be to share the secret with my sister. After all, Marianne's vortex of overdramatic romantic disappointment was getting increasingly irritating. I'd have jumped at the tiniest chance of shutting her down by offering up my own, even more horrific, dilemma for comparison.

Once again, Austen's depiction of Elinor's mute anguish is likely to connect with modern women through shared experiences. Readers (and Elinor) realize that Lucy Steele is manipulating her. Nevertheless, Elinor keeps silent. Despite her close relationship with Marianne, she doesn't disclose her pain. Rachel Simmons would find Elinor's behavior typical, as her research indicates that "anger is rarely articulated" between young women. Simmons explains that behind the "facade of female intimacy lies a terrain traveled in secret, marked with anguish, and nourished by silence." Western culture expects girls to be good. Showing anger, Simmons argues, would undermine "who girls have been raised to become."

In their work on human behavior in the digital age, "The Positivity Bias and Prosocial Deception on Facebook," communication experts Erin Spottswood and Jeffrey Hancock refer to this type of conduct as "positive face concern." Humans tend to project positive emotions, preferring to keep personal struggles private. Elinor demonstrates face-saving behavior throughout the novel, concealing her real feelings to preserve her dignity and "avoid damaging the sensibility of others."

Secret still intact, Elinor and Marianne manage to escape the oppressive presence of the Steeles by joining Mrs. Jennings in London. To their dismay, Lucy and her sister follow them there, the fruit of their ingratiation campaign. "Even though Lucy was not elegant, and her sister not even genteel," they had made themselves so agreeable that Lady Middleton asks them to spend a week or two in their London home.

Unsurprisingly, Elinor was not amused.

WE AREN'T ALL FRIENDS

That their host is oblivious to the hostility between Elinor and Lucy is typical of female indirect aggression, even today. "All these jealousies and discontents," Austen relates, "were so totally unsuspected by Mrs. Jennings." We learn that the ever-hopeful matriarch thinks "it a delightful thing for the girls to be together."

One positive lesson from Elinor's secret-keeping is that silence can be just as damaging as gossip. Elinor denies Lucy a valid, socially recognized reason to hate her by remaining tight-lipped. Instead, Lucy is forced to aggress more and more overtly, never failing to "inform her confidante of her happiness whenever she received a letter from Edward." Elinor refuses to satisfy Lucy's hunger for confirmation by failing to react. It's only us, Elinor's readers, who witness her inner pain, despite her outer calm. "As soon as civility would allow," we learn that Elinor dismisses Lucy's news. She feels that "such conversations were an indulgence which Lucy did not deserve, and which were dangerous to herself."

And so, the two young women spend their time in London exchanging fabrications. Lucy pretends that Miss Dashwood is her ally, and Elinor plays at being unaffected. Knowing that the situation saddens her rival, Lucy probes, "Are you ill, Miss Dashwood?—you seem low—you don't speak;—sure you an't well." We witness Elinor struggling to remain calm in the face of Lucy's exuberance and poor language. "I am perfectly convinced of your regard for me, and next to Edward's love, it is the greatest comfort I have," Lucy coos. Heaping on the bullshit, she adds, "heaven knows what I should have done without your friendship."

It's not surprising when Lucy drops her all-important buddy as soon as the truth comes out, and Regency readers were not likely shocked by Edward's resulting disinheritance. As Lynda Hall explains, while "some movement within the social ranks" was allowed, "obvious social climbers were maligned." Hall elaborates, adding that "even though a marriage between a woman like the nearly penniless Lucy and a man like the potentially wealthy Edward Ferrars was possible," the pair would receive little to no social support for such a drastic leap on the economic scale. Hall posits that "Lucy, therefore, must be sly in her attempt to create the perception of expressed value" from her natural place "on the margin of genteel society."

Clever Lucy manages just that. She maneuvers her way back into favor reasonably quickly after marrying Edward's brother, Robert. With "perseverance in humility of conduct and messages, in self-condemnation for Robert's offense, and gratitude for the unkindness she was treated with," aka *sucking up*, Lucy eventually reverses the situation. Finally, she gets "the haughty notice which overcame her by its graciousness, and led soon afterwards, by rapid degrees, to the highest state of affection and influence." In the end, "Lucy became as necessary to Mrs. Ferrars as either Robert or Fanny."

Anyone seeking Lucy's comeuppance closes *Sense and Sensibility* sadly disappointed. Although both Elinor and Marianne marry their own Prince Charmings in the end, any sense of victory is dampened by the fact that the scheming Lucy manages the same. Hers is not a cautionary tale. Instead, it drives home the reality that then—as now—virtue alone is not enough to ensure success. There is no such thing as a purely happy ending like in real life. Instead of being a warning to ambitious gold diggers, Hall sees "the whole of Lucy's behavior in the affair, and the prosperity which crowned it," to be "a most encouraging instance of what an earnest, an unceasing attention to self-interest," can provide for a young woman. By investing a bit of "time and conscience," a girl could secure "every advantage of fortune." Lucy is rewarded for her actions, which can only compare negatively to Elinor's wholesome principles.

If success in Austen is purely a trip to the altar with a single man in possession of a good fortune, Lucy wins.

But does she?

Predicting modern self-help books on real happiness, decluttering, and the life-affirming power of HGTV and redecorating, Austen describes Elinor and Edward as "one of the happiest couples in the world." Although not wealthy, they have "an income quite sufficient to their wants." On top of that, their patron Colonel Brandon picks up the tab for new wallpaper and improved curb appeal for the parsonage in Delaford.

The biggest prize of them all?

Elinor is finally relieved from "the persecution of Lucy's friendship."

Part II

A HEROINE WHOM
NO ONE WILL MUCH LIKE

CHAPTER 4

A State of Warfare with Augusta Elton

Sometimes it seems as if her creatures were born merely to give
Jane Austen the supreme delight of slicing their heads off.
—VIRGINIA WOOLF

Early Austen critics complained that despite living in a time marked almost invariably by war, the author didn't address it directly. How dare she, the daughter of a parochial clergyman, not write about the most significant issues facing the men of her era? How did this female author, with little formal education, shunted from village to town and back again according to the whims of male relatives, not address battles with Napoleon or trouble in the colonies? Those critics fail to recognize that Austen outlined skirmishes of another kind—ongoing hostilities between her female characters.

Austen's life was filled with the repercussions of war, if not the battles themselves. She had two brothers in the military and a relative guillotined in France. With that in mind, can we continue to ignore that she chose the term "warfare" to describe relations between women? After all, her fourth novel, *Emma*, is rife with micro-aggressive confrontations between its heroine and the new girl in town.

Since its publication, the novel has been the subject of copious literary criticism and extravagantly personal reader response. The story's clueless title character has been reincarnated numerous times in film, manga comics, and fanfiction, never seeming to grow old. The public and scholars alike unite in finding Emma manipulative yet charming; Austen herself thought her problematic. According to her nephew, Austen began the work stating, "I am going to take a heroine whom no-one but myself will much like."

BAD CAN BE GOOD AND GOOD CAN BE BAD

Liked or not, Austen captures incredibly authentic human behavior in her depiction of Emma Woodhouse. Austen's contemporary, Scottish novelist Susan Ferrier, recounted her impressions. "The heroine is no better than other people," she remarked, "but the characters are all so true to life, and the style so piquant that it does not require the adventitious aids of mystery and adventure." Likewise, early Austen biographer Mrs. Charles Malden calls Emma Woodhouse "very good." Malden considers "her faults, follies, and mistakes" to be precisely those "of a warm-hearted, rather spoilt girl, accustomed to believe in herself and to be the queen of her own circle." She contemplates that Emma fully "deserves the amount of punishment she gets, but we are glad that it is no worse."

Today's Janeites feel the same. My online survey of hundreds of avid Austen readers shows that they are fully aware that Emma isn't a conventional heroine. One participant calls Emma "deeply flawed, but fun." Another adds that "sometimes I love her, sometimes I'm horrified by her," summing up the overindulged girl as "exasperating but likable." Oddly enough, despite all her flaws, female readers expressed significantly more affection for egocentric Emma than for Fanny Price, arguably Austen's most (annoyingly) well-behaved protagonist.

As for me? I am not a fan of Emma Woodhouse.

That might surprise some people. Readers who have already flipped through this book will have noticed that I've dedicated three whole chapters to the perplexingly misguided heroine.

What gives?

My feelings about Emma remind me of what Mark Twain wrote about Austen. "Her books madden me so," he complained, adding, "I can't conceal my frenzy." He admitted that "every time" he read Austen, he felt compelled "to dig her up and beat her over the skull with her own shin-bone."

If his hatred was real, there would not be an "every time."

While I'm not a proponent of bone-based violence, Emma does drive me nuts *every time* I read her. Still, I'd never dream of stopping. She's become a familiar (albeit messed-up) old friend.

Reading *Emma* is like watching someone pull the wings off flies.

It's hard to get upset about flies, but it still seems cruel and unnecessary. What business do we humans have, destroying an insect's life? Is wing-pulling a tonic for boredom? Is it a learning experience? Is it about testing ways of treating people or just some strange kind of fun?

DON'T MESS WITH PEOPLE JUST BECAUSE YOU CAN

For me, Emma Woodhouse is literature's most excellent fly-wing puller. From her position of well-heeled, relative safety, she feels free to mess up the women's lives around her, from harmless schoolgirl Harriet Smith to impoverished spinster Miss Bates. Is she justified in her behavior? Just as much as anyone with a penchant for pulling wings off flies.

Not at all.

In animal behavior terms, Emma is Highbury's alpha girl, the fortunate beneficiary of pretty much anything a girl could want. She lives in a big house near a large village, in a neighborhood which "afforded her no equals." She never questions her own authority and is rarely challenged. As soon as her sister marries and leaves town, she becomes the mistress of her father's house, relishing being the focus of attention when her father can be distracted from his hypochondria. Her closest intimate is her former governess, over whom Emma has had the upper hand from an early age. No wonder Emma feels entitled to do whatever she likes. Why shouldn't she?

Change is in the air when Emma loses her beloved Miss Taylor to marriage, an event Emma credits herself for orchestrating. Delighted by the misguided notion of being a matchmaker, Emma attempts to unite her muddle-headed friend Harriet with the town's eligible rector, Mr. Elton. Inconceivably to Emma, the man has other ideas. Not interested in an orphan of uncertain parentage, he'd like to marry Emma herself. He quickly recovers from her rejection by selecting a young lady from out of town, the wealthy and attractive Miss Augusta Hawkins. Following the "a stranger comes to town" trope, competition and cattiness ensue as the new girl makes her way in village society. With Augusta's arrival, Emma is suddenly no longer Highbury's only shining star of wealthy femininity. To cope, our hapless heroine dissects the perceived interloper, searching for weakness and pulling off her wings.

What do readers know about the vicar's new wife? Although Hollywood versions frequently depict her as an oddball, Austen is clear: the new Mrs. Elton is charming, beautiful, and—even more important for Mr. Elton—has 10,000 pounds to her name. After just a few glorious "smiles and blushes," she (and her cash) snags him quickly during his escape to Bath.

Her crime toward Miss Woodhouse? She arrives in Highbury with just a little too much self-confidence for Emma's taste. Within a few minutes of meeting Augusta, Emma resolves that "she did not really like her." Emma declares her vain, overly satisfied with herself, and determined to shine. The new Mrs. Elton was "pert and familiar."

How dare she!

Austen assures readers that Emma relishes her distaste. She doesn't waste a moment gathering accurate impressions of the new girl (or practicing her pianoforte or improving her drawing abilities, for that matter). Instead, our illogical heroine spends a "long, very long" time occupying herself with all of Mrs. Elton's imagined "offenses." Where exactly does this instinctual rivalry come from? Augusta hasn't done anything to harm Emma or her sidekick Harriet; that notion is purely in Emma's head.

ALLIES ARE EXISTENTIAL

The work of evolutionary psychology professor Joyce F. Benenson provides clues. In her meta-analysis of various studies on female intra-gender aggression among both human and nonhuman primates, Benenson identifies a set of five common behaviors. She finds that these manifest throughout the developmental phases of our lives, beginning as early as toddlerhood. The list includes:

1. A tendency to avoid direct, physical harm to other girls to protect ourselves
2. Enforcing equality in our peer group
3. Using social exclusion to hurt others
4. Masking the intent to injure
5. Only competing openly if our status is higher than that of our victims.

Benenson traces the origins of each of these mechanisms in her work, "The Development of Human Female Competition: Allies and Adversaries." She links these behaviors back to a simple evolutionary need to provide for ourselves and our offspring regardless of age.

Evolutionary psychology is a relatively new scientific discipline that began gaining traction in the 1990s. Of course, it's not about inviting Neanderthals or prehistoric *homo sapiens* to lie on a couch and talk about their relationship with their mothers. Instead, evolutionary psychologists apply findings from various sources to understand the evolutionary and genetic development of the human mind over time. These include human and animal behavior studies, physical and cultural anthropology, developmental psychology, neuroscience, economics, and sociology. They work on the basic assumption that, like all other organisms, humans also continue to evolve through genetic mutation or one of two primary mechanisms: natural or sexual selection.

What does this have to do with Jane Austen and the power struggle between Emma and Augusta? Because almost everything the author wrote reflects the very human drive to protect our genetic heritage, albeit under the guise of holy matrimony.

Let me show you.

Benenson argues that whether we realize it or not, our need to preserve our genes can lead to female intra-gender competition. Even before we consider having children, we instinctually work to preserve ourselves and our female kin, and with that, our DNA.

Historically, women have relied on their female relatives to support each other during gestation, childbirth, and childrearing. After all, no matter how clever and rich the Emma Woodhouses of the world are, they still need honest advice about breastfeeding and how to soothe a colicky baby. Although it was conceivable that women like Emma could outsource these tasks to a wet nurse or nanny, she still could very realistically die in childbirth. She must trust that this small circle of women would take care of her infant should the worst come to pass.

Citing numerous studies, Benenson posits that only certain women can fulfill such roles. In study after study across 173 different cultures, Benenson finds that "girls and women still view parents and parental substitutes as more important than an unrelated close friend for providing both instrumental and emotional assistance." No matter how much Emma dallies with lower-status Harriet Smith, the character has only two real female intimates: her sister Isabella and her ersatz-mother, Mrs. Weston. Both are gentlewomen and figures of absolute trust. Unlike Harriet Smith, they can be depended on to provide sustenance and shelter for Emma's children should she not be able to. In return, they can expect the same from her.

Although most of us would probably describe ourselves as altruistic, Benenson finds very little evidence of readiness to perform such duties for women outside of our close communities. There isn't much to gain in evolutionary terms by investing in them. Instead, there is much to be lost, from access to physical resources, social standing, or access to potential mates and helpmeets.

Please don't shoot the messenger.

THERE'S NO JANE AUSTEN FIGHT CLUB

One (questionably) positive behavior Benenson cites is most women's aversion to physically harming their rivals. While not many are ready to care for strange women's offspring, we are equally unenthusiastic about causing bodily harm. This might explain why women's boxing has remained controversial, considered by many to be a sport for the male gaze.

The expected unlikeliness of women's physical aggression has led to female misogyny receiving little attention until recent decades, as it can be tough to spot. In contrast, it's hard *not* to see two boys hitting each other; loud "roughhousing" feels expected. Although there is some evidence of female-on-female harm in Austen, she certainly doesn't condone physical violence. It could be argued that sending Jane Bennet out in the rain and withholding a fire from Fanny Price's room are acts of abuse, but they aren't committed in ways that could harm the perpetrator should they fail. If we want to get all evolutionary about it, Jane's illness likely *accelerated* the propagation of Mrs. Bennet's genetic goods. The pity Fanny receives from her cousin lays the foundation for their later union. Most women can't afford to tussle with their enemies; we have enough on our plates already.

Emma's hatred of Augusta is evident to us, her readers. For those around her, it is subtle and harder to identify.

Just what is Emma's problem, anyway?

Augusta Elton behaves as if she were special.

WOE TO THE WOMAN WHO TRIES TO APPEAR BETTER THAN OTHERS

"Within the female community," Benenson writes, "girls reduce competition by demanding equality." Those who "openly attempt to attain more than others" are punished in ways so subtle and disguised that even the perpetrators aren't aware of what they are doing. Girls are constantly comparing themselves to each other and are wary of befriending a girl whom they see as being any way better or worse than them and their peers.

Worryingly, this behavior starts exceptionally early. Benenson observed three-year-old toddlers enforcing a sense of equality among their playmates. Even at that tender age, Benenson claims, "a girl cannot assert her social power or superiority as an individual without risking other girls' denigration." Augusta Elton walks a fine line in knowing her worth as a self-assured, cosmopolitan young woman and being accepted in local society.

In keeping with Benenson's research, Austen depicts Augusta as demurring when it's essential. After all, young women like the new Mrs. Elton are expected to remain humble and self-effacing, at least in the eyes of their female peers. Augusta is clearly aware of her own value yet carefully couches her words in comparisons to avoid seeming boastful. Austen masters this by showing Augusta likening her brother-in-law's estate to Mr. Woodhouse's. Droning on and on about its similarity to Maple Grove, "Mr. Suckling's seat," and appealing to her husband for confirmation of its "astonishing" likeness, Mrs. Elton cunningly informs Emma of her family's affluence.

What she doesn't reckon with is Emma's immediate, internal declaration that she is "a vain woman." Within minutes, Emma finds Mrs. Elton (unacceptably) "extremely well satisfied with herself," "thinking much of her own importance," and disturbingly anxious "to shine and be very superior." Not only has Augusta Elton failed to disguise her competitive nature, but she also appears to think more highly of herself than much of Highbury society.

By the time Augusta senses Emma's aversion, it's too late. She attempts to mitigate the damage by doubling down on affiliative speech, peppering her dialogue with positive-sounding phrases, cooing "I perfectly understand your situation," and "I assure you." "I am delighted to find myself in such a circle," she fawns, referring to Emma as "dear Miss Woodhouse." When this doesn't succeed, her words become stealthy weapons, aimed at emotional rather than physical distress.

Finding herself rebuffed, Augusta eventually begins to passive-aggressively bait Emma. Recognizing that Emma has seen little of the outside world, she pretends to instruct Miss Woodhouse on the glories of Bath. Under the pretext of kindness and generosity, she gushes about its health benefits, humble-bragging that she could "immediately secure" introductions to some of the best society in the spa town, should Emma venture to go.

Despite being couched as a generous offer, Emma bristles at her audacious claim. Acceptance would position Augusta above Emma in the role of benefactor. "It was as much as Emma could bear, without being impolite," Austen reports. "She was revolted by the notion that she would be indebted to Mrs. Elton for what was called an introduction." Just as Benenson would predict, her response is full of scorn. "The dignity of Miss Woodhouse, of Hartfield, was sunk indeed!" "Insufferable woman!" Emma tells herself. "Worse than I had supposed. Absolutely insufferable!"

KEEP YOUR HOSTILITY TO YOURSELF
(BUT YOU PROBABLY ALREADY KNEW THAT)

It's obvious to readers that Emma hasn't given Augusta a real chance to be her friend. Despite declaring to herself that she "would not be in a hurry to find fault," Emma quickly dismisses the vicar's wife. Austen alerts us that Emma "suspected that there was no elegance;—ease, but not elegance." Within minutes, she was "almost sure that for a young woman, a stranger, a bride, there was too much ease."

Interestingly, Austen describes Emma attempting to couch her hostility in benign undertones even in her inner dialogue. Following Benenson, it's no wonder. Expectations of "niceness and equality remain the female community's norms," she tells us. The primary justification one girl gives for being mean to another? She is acting superior.

Instead of calling Augusta rude names, our heroine considers that "her person was rather good; her face not unpretty." Still, Austen makes it clear that Emma is in no way inclined to like the interloper, as "neither feature, nor air, nor voice, nor manner, were elegant." Critically important for our evaluation of Emma is Austen's clarification that "Emma thought at least it would turn out so."

In line with Benenson's findings, Emma employs subtle, silent means to block Augusta's social ascent. "Within the female community," Benenson concludes, "girls reduce competition by demanding equality and punishing those who openly attempt to attain more than others." "Even in the rare girl gangs that exist," Benenson notes, "the leader must behave as an equal."

Augusta doesn't quite manage this, boasting as she does about Mr. Suckling's Regency-equivalent of a Lamborghini. By repeatedly referencing his private barouche landau, she obliquely defines the socioeconomic bracket she is used to inhabiting.

Austen never lets us doubt precisely what is going on. Accessing Augusta's thoughts, we know that she was ready for Mr. Woodhouse to escort her into the dining room first as propriety and precedence expected. Nevertheless, she feigns feminine hesitancy, half questioning, "must I go first?" although she damn well knows the answer. Disingenuously, she alleges, "I really am ashamed of always leading the way."

In other scenes, Augusta pretends modesty. After investing several moments admiring Jane Fairfax's dress and appearance, "Mrs. Elton was evidently wanting to be complimented" herself. Confronted with silence, she is forced to ask what others think of her gown and hair, sharing that "my friends say I am not entirely devoid of taste." She immediately realizes the impact of her words and that she is entering dangerous territory in girl terms.

According to professor emerita of psychology and women's studies, Phyllis Chesler, girls are constantly scrutinizing each other for "displays that might be interpreted as showing that one girl is trying to differentiate herself from others in the group." Any girl interpreted to be status-seeking will find herself quickly rejected or excluded by her peers. Mrs. Elton quickly attempts to mitigate her faux pas, adding, "nobody can think less of dress in general than I do." In case this wasn't quite enough, Mrs. Elton frames her need for praise as a social convention intended to honor her hosts. "In compliment to the Westons," she explains, "who I have no doubt are giving this ball chiefly to do me honor," Mrs. Elton claims that she would not "wish to be inferior to others."

It's pretty normal for girls like Emma to want to punish others attempting to hog the spotlight, and I do not doubt that Austen intends for us to understand that both Emma and Mrs. Elton are hyperaware of each other's every move.

Emma determines that "when they had nothing else to say, it must be always easy to begin abusing Miss Woodhouse." Convinced that she's the center of the Highbury universe, Emma decides that the pair could not overtly disrespect her due to her status. Instead, Emma is sure that they find "a broader vent in contemptuous treatment of Harriet." Somehow, Emma feels that the Eltons were "sneering and negligent" toward the girl, to the point of being "unpleasant."

I'm not 100 percent sure I blame her. I don't know about you, but my instinct at parties is not to focus on schoolgirls with whom I have nothing in common. It may not be noble or generous, but I choose to spend my time getting to know people with whom I might have a connection. As the wife of the town's clergyman, I'd expect Mrs. Elton to invest her time with prominent members of the community, not some little twit, no matter how tragic her circumstances.

Mrs. Elton behaves just as Benenson would likely predict; she excludes Harriet from the conversation. The tactic is common, representing for Benenson "a safe strategy for increasing physical resources, allies, and status opportunities by decreasing the number of competitors." Emma gets this. She knows that regardless of how unfair it may seem, the vicar's wife simply can't retaliate against a social equal, but what she *may* do is ignore Harriet Smith.

CHAPTER 4

BE A GRACIOUS GUEST

Austen certainly understood the negative impact of social exclusion. Early in the novel, Emma experiences it herself. Learning of a dinner party to be held by the Coles, a family active in the (then) degrading business of trade, Emma assumes that she won't be invited, or if she is, her status in the community would force her to decline. After all, her family is far superior to theirs. Readers watch Emma pen theoretical replies to their presumptuous (nonexistent) invitation. Once again, assuming herself to be the focus of the entire town, Emma's thoughts reflect her superficiality. "The Coles were very respectable in their way," she thinks, "but they ought to be taught that it was not for them to arrange the terms on which the superior families would visit them."

Ironically, Emma's snobbishness backfires, and Austen punishes her for it. Everyone receives an invitation, *except* Emma and her father. Suddenly, the once derided event becomes a much coveted one. Forced to reevaluate, Emma eagerly accepts the request when it finally does arrive.

She is similarly surprised to find herself excluded from a gathering after the fateful excursion to Box Hill. "You spent the evening with Mrs. Elton?" Emma asks Miss Bates, having passed the same hours sadly alone with her invalid father. Gentle Miss Bates makes it clear that the snub was intentional. Chatting away as she always does, Miss Bates asserts that Mrs. Elton insisted that the entire group attend (sans Emma).

In an oblique reference to the spoiled girl's joke at her expense, Miss Bates continues. "My mother, and Jane, and I, were all there, and a very agreeable evening we had." "I shall always think it a very pleasant party," she gushes, adding that she felt "extremely obliged to the kind friends who included me in it."

The same could *not* be said of her time on Box Hill.

DON'T LET BOX HILL BE THE ONE YOU DIE ON

A word to the wise? Stay away from Box Hill. The very words "Box Hill" are enough to inspire secondhand mortification in every sensitive Janeite. The gist of the outing? Two vain young women went up a hill, and one came tumbling down disgraced.

It's the events at Box Hill that finally enable Mrs. Elton to be rid of Emma without social repercussions. Austen lays Emma's fallibility bare at the legendary picnic. Even before setting foot into the carriage, which will convey her to the famous lookout point, Emma dreads the day. She has never been to Box Hill and intends to visit it with a few chosen friends, "in a quiet, unpretending, elegant way," which was "infinitely superior to the bustle and preparation, the regular eating and drinking, and picnic parade" of people like the Eltons.

She is disappointed to learn that her hosts for the journey had included the Eltons in the party. Since she couldn't remind them of her "very great dislike" of Mrs. Elton, she was "obliged to consent to an arrangement which she would have done a great deal to avoid." Why? It's "an arrangement which would probably expose her even to the degradation of being said to be of Mrs. Elton's party!" Drama queen Emma convinces herself that her "every feeling was offended."

Both young women swell at the idea of the other "presiding" over the outing. Frank Churchill, that selfish fool, backs Emma. Mrs. Elton is endorsed by her marital state, attempting to level the playing field by declaring herself chaperone.

On Box Hill, we realize that we've been duped. Since the beginning of the novel, Austen has managed to repress our niggling doubts about Emma. Surrounded by strawberries and sunshine, we can no longer ignore her true, very fallible nature.

Emma Woodhouse is a mean girl.

Our self-indulgent heroine expects everyone to entertain her. She resents Frank Churchill's silence and finds both him and Harriet "dull" and "insufferable." Only after Frank made her "his first object" does she reconcile herself to the outing. She is "glad to be enlivened, not sorry to be flattered." Although she has no genuine interest in Frank as a beau, she flirts with him shamelessly, knowing full well that their behavior is reproachable.

Mrs. Elton sensibly declines to engage in the juvenile and "silly games" that Frank proposes. Her refusal is entirely in keeping with societal expectations of a clergyman's wife, which Emma conveniently forgets. She injures an innocent bystander, the gabby yet endearing Miss Bates, in her constant efforts to monopolize attention.

"Emma could not resist."

She makes an offhand remark, driving a knife in the spinster's soft, warm heart.

I dread the scene every time I read it. Like everything Miss Bates does, she absorbs the message by talking it through. "I must make myself very disagreeable, or she would not have said such a thing to an old friend," the unsettled woman worries.

Emma's lack of impulse control effectively ends the doomed party; Mrs. Elton promptly flees the scene with her husband, followed by Mr. Knightley, Miss Bates, and Miss Fairfax.

Literary scholar Terry Castle describes the scene aptly. "What is disturbing about the Box Hill episode," she writes, "is that it intimates, momentarily, a world in disorder and a 'principle of separation' at work in human affairs." For an instant, "civility itself seems to break down, and the novel verges on nightmare." By baiting Miss Bates, Castle declares, Emma "bears more than a passing resemblance to the scapegoating rituals of primitive societies, in which the weakest member of the group is selected for sacrifice." "As Emma is taken off in the carriage, more miserable than 'at any circumstance in her life,'" Castle continues, "we sense Austen tapping into certain primal human fears—of abandonment, of violent expulsion from the group, of being sent away to die."

Castle concludes that "when Austen's smarty-pants heroine loses patience with dotty old Miss Bates," she earns a deservedly harsh rebuke from Mr. Knightley. The scene shows that "yes, some old ladies are appallingly out of it, but you damn well better not be cruel to them if you want to live with yourself afterward."

Like pulling the wings off a fly, Emma abuses Miss Bates simply because she *can*.

After Box Hill, it becomes impossible to ignore Emma's serious flaws. Even *she* eventually realizes that her behavior is atrocious. More startling than her terrible comment is learning that we have been complicit in Emma's antics. Like the fate of a single, dissected fly, Emma's statement on Box Hill is a tiny thing. And yet, as Virginia Woolf explains, Austen "stimulates us to supply what is not there."

On the surface, most of what Austen offers her readers could be considered as trifles: quaint manners, group outings, and chaste courtship. Not true, according to Woolfe. In truth, Austen's words are "composed of something that expands in the reader's mind and endows the most enduring form of life scenes which are outwardly trivial."

There is no "battle" of Box Hill.

There are no corpses or smoking guns left on the picnic blanket.

And yet, in just a few brief paragraphs, Austen has turned a molehill into a mountain. Emma has never "felt so agitated, mortified, grieved, at any circumstance in her life." Mr. Knightley admonishes her, demanding compassion for Miss Bates instead of ridicule. "She is poor," Knightley emphasizes, and "has sunk from the comforts she was born to." He reminds Emma of the real hardships other unmarried women face; not everyone is a wealthy Woodhouse. Miss Bates can only sink further.

Finally, Emma takes her head out of her own pampered behind. There is no denying the truth of Mr. Knightley's words. She is "most forcibly struck." "She felt it at her heart. How could she have been so brutal, so cruel to Miss Bates!"

Oh, Miss Austen, fashioning Emma's thoughts as an exclamation, not a question!

In these tiny, seemingly minuscule details, I believe Austen *still sees* *us* two centuries later. She knows that all of us are in our way mean girls, and she loves us for it. It would not do to describe Augusta Elton merely in terms of generous deeds. She must be awful in some way to be authentic. Perfectly nice people are exhausting. No wonder Austen told her sister, "I do not want people to be very agreeable, as it saves me the trouble of liking them a great deal."

Until this point in the novel, Austen has encouraged us to renounce Mrs. Elton and her performative-seeming charity. Emma certainly does; she's annoyed when Augusta declares herself "Lady Patroness" to the Bates ladies, conveniently forgetting Mrs. Elton's role in the church community. Instead, our misguided main character resents the new bride's perpetual "praise, encouragement, and offers of service." It's doubtful that Austen, herself a clergyman's daughter, was apt to forget what society expected of a vicar's wife.

Consider this: Emma spends the evening after Box Hill absorbed in herself, stewing in narcissistic remorse. When she rushes to apologize to Miss Bates the following day, she isn't thinking of her victim; rather, if Mr. Knightley will be there to witness it. "Her eyes were on Donwell as she walked, but she saw him not."

Mrs. Elton might appear ostentatious, yet she spends the same hours welcoming Miss Bates, her mother, and her niece into her home, providing them with "a very agreeable evening." She leverages her contacts to do something objectively very generous, identifying a safe, respectable, well-paid position for their beloved Miss Fairfax. While a career as a governess isn't exactly Jane's dream, the offer and the action represent significantly kindhearted deeds in a Regency context.

Once again, Austen challenges us to question everything! Of course, we expect the book's title character to be a flawless heroine. Instead, Emma Woodhouse is human and fallible, and her defensiveness toward the arrival of a stranger in town is a normal part of the human experience. In Austen, black is never *truly* black, and white often is a shade of gray.

Austen doesn't let us forget just how ordinary both young women are. At the end, when Harriet Smith is safely spoken for and Jane Fairfax has neatly avoided servitude, the two remain rivals. After three acts, Emma still feels free to leave Mrs. Elton off her wedding guest list, including only a "small band of true friends."

For her part, Augusta declares the event "extremely shabby, and very inferior to her own."

It's not hard to imagine the pair growing old together in unfailing dislike, relishing feelings of silent superiority over one another from the safety of their family pews.

CHAPTER 5

Emma Woodhouse

A Disposition to Think a Little Too Well of Herself

> Why should Caesar get to stomp around like a giant while the
> rest of us try not to get smushed under his big feet? What's so
> great about Caesar, hm? Brutus is just as cute as Caesar. Brutus is
> just as smart as Caesar; people totally like Brutus as much as they
> like Caesar. WE SHOULD TOTALLY JUST STAB CAESAR!
> —Gretchen Wieners, *Mean Girls*

Every high school seems to have them: unspoken yet clearly defined hierarchies of perceived coolness. At my rural alma mater, the lightly athletic types prevailed. There were no bulky muscles or protective gear for them; they were the cheerleaders in pleated skirts and perky pony-tails. They lived in subdivisions, not trailer parks. They had fathers who worked in offices, not in factories or farms. They knew how to play American sports, the kind that foreign-born dads like mine had never learned.

Of course, my assumptions were ridiculous. As an adult, I realized that the only person's life I truly know is mine alone. Those girls' places at the pinnacle of high school's elite were entirely in my imagination.

The only thing I *can* be sure of is my envy at the time. Those girls seemed to do everything better; they could conform, fit in, shine. They always seemed to know just what to say and do. They always had friends to sit with in the cafeteria and dates to the dance.

What made them seem invincible? They were never alone.

It's the same with Emma Woodhouse. When her former governess and chaperone, Miss Taylor, leaves to establish her own home, Emma needn't do much to replace her. With a snip of her fingers, she chooses a new friend, the unsophisticated and malleable Harriet Smith. Together with Harriet, Emma happily spends her days progressing through the village, visiting, passing judgment, and believing herself to be a matchmaker. A member of the upper crust, Emma assumes her right to the Harriets of the world. For her, friends are a form of entertainment, a welcome diversion, a leisure activity far more satisfying than needlework or sketching.

Emma has the luxury of choice.

In our world, girls like Emma Woodhouse never sit alone in the cafeteria.

The same sense of privilege that empowers Emma to criticize Augusta Elton allows her the pick of new friends. No television? No internet? No Mrs. Weston? The neighborhood ladies' school is a one-stop-shop for fresh, compliant companionship. Since friends are entertainment, she isn't vested in being a great friend herself. She cloaks her misguided actions in country walks, invitations to tea, and terrible advice. Emma need not worry that hanging out with her does more harm than good; she firmly believes that spending time with sweet, young Harriet is a charity rather than corruption.

"The real evils, indeed, of Emma's situation," the narrator tells us, was "the power of having rather too much her own way and a disposition to think a little too well of herself." Unlike Jane Fairfax and Harriet Smith, Emma has a fortune; she can afford to do whatever she likes.

FRIENDSHIPS EVOLVE

In the last chapter, Joyce Benenson's examination of a broad array of social scientific findings from almost two hundred cultures showed that intense female camaraderie is an essential part of social interaction. It's no wonder, then, that female relationships have been a popular narrative trope since writing began. In Greek mythology, the legendary Amazon warriors banded together, rebelling against a male-dominated world. No men lived among them; they allowed them into their lives for procreation once a year. Male babies didn't fare well—they were either killed or left to die from exposure.

Ruth sticks to her mother-in-law Naomi's side in the Judeo-Christian Bible, refusing to abandon her on her trek back to Bethlehem. Shakespeare is replete with female pairs relying on each other through thick and thin, from Rosalind and Celia in *As You Like It* fleeing a menacing patriarch together to cousins Hero and Beatrice of *Much Ado About Nothing* faking death to catch a (way too judgmental) man.

Benenson's explanation of such bonds as powerful support in reproductive success may seem a bit visceral to Western audiences. The twentieth century brought many advances in women's rights, and most of us enjoy (albeit shrinking) choices over our bodies and careers. We live in a day and age slowly recognizing that being a woman doesn't always correspond to what is written on our birth certificates. We are free to enter romantic or platonic friendships with whomever we want. We can pay others to mind and even bear our offspring. We no longer need to rely solely on our female kin or friends to ensure the safety of our genetic goods.

Nevertheless, friendship still *feels* essential for most of us.

Looking back at those horrible high school days, I don't remember attending a single social event *without* a good girlfriend. Some girls traveled in packs, some in pairs. Being with friends turned visits to the ladies' room into impromptu gossip sessions, opportunities to determine who was cute, who was best avoided, and who had lipstick on their teeth. I'd love to claim that the decisions I made at the time were based on facts and intellect, but it was my friends who influenced me the most. We dressed alike. We listened to the same music. We experimented with the world alike.

Don't judge me.

I'd bet Austen felt the same. Her favorite person in life was her sister, Cassandra. When they weren't together, she wrote long letters to her, recounting time spent at balls, on walks, and staying up until late in the night with another woman, their mutual friend Martha. Their relationship was significant for both Austen girls. In one message to Cassandra, Austen describes Martha as a "friend and sister under every circumstance."

Regency conduct books had much to say about close female relationships. Since at least the Middle Ages, conduct books aimed at young women have attempted to educate them in acceptable morals and behavior. Austen herself read Thomas Ghisborne's *An Enquiry in the Duties of the Female Sex*, which outlined a broad range of subjects from selecting a spouse to raising children.

In *Jane Austen among Women*, English professor Deborah Kaplan suggests that female friendship provided powerful psychological support to young women of the time. Although companionship among women propped up the popular image of domestic femininity, eighteenth-century conduct books advised women to focus on their families first.

While conduct books preached primary allegiance to family, Regency novels describe a much different situation. In her book *Women's Friendships in Literature*, scholar Janet Todd points out that fictional mothers of the time tend to be "usually bad and living or good and dead." It's hard to argue when looking at Mrs. Bennet, Lady Bertram, Lady Catherine, or even the missing Elliot and Woodhouse mothers. The sensible, understanding older women in Austen's narratives are never the protagonist's mother; they are aunts or family friends—which may have been true for Austen herself.

After her father's passing, Austen's adult household was made up solely of women. Pooling resources with her mother, Cassandra, and Martha, Austen scraped by on a limited income. She relied heavily on her sister and friend to ensure she had the peace of mind and personal space needed to focus on her writing. In part, we have them to thank for the six wonderful novels Austen put into the world.

WE NEED EACH OTHER

Emma Woodhouse also relies on her female peers, turning to her older sister or former governess in serious matters. As the novel opens, Emma needs a distraction, not a true confidante. Harriet emerges onto the scene just as Emma is on the lookout for a new pal. What do we know about her? Only that "someone" paid for her education and that she is pleasant to look at.

Emma and Harriet's first meeting could come straight out of Rosalind Wiseman's bestselling parenting book, *Queen Bees and Wannabes,* introduced in the first chapter. In it, Wiseman aggregates years of behavioral research. Mapping out the hierarchy of high schools, Wiseman reports that charismatic, manipulative personalities like Emma Woodhouse are a common commodity.

Similarly, Austen delineates Highbury's social order when describing the list of welcome visitors at Hartfield. At the pinnacle are the Westons, Mr. Knightley, and Mr. Elton. "After these came a second set," made up of Mrs. Bates and her daughter and the local schoolmistress, Mrs. Goddard. These ladies are considered by the Woodhouses as the "most come-at-able," generally willing and able to attend to the Highbury set at the drop of a hat. Mrs. Bates is a respectable vicar's widow, and her daughter has the good sense of not being threatening in any way. Miss Bates is neither intelligent, beautiful, nor wealthy; she is happy in her place in the world and doesn't "frighten those who might hate her."

Similarly, Mrs. Goddard is described as plain and motherly, running a "real, honest, old-fashioned boarding school" from which no girl emerged as a vain prodigy. "These were the ladies whom Emma found herself very frequently able to collect," Austen tells us. Her words are remarkably like Wiseman's, who finds that girls like Emma tend to surround themselves with carefully vetted "Wannabes."

In Wiseman's terms, Emma is a quintessential teenage Queen Bee, like Isabella Thorpe before her. Where Isabella employs her age and experience as leverage, Emma unconsciously exploits the money, looks, and power that life has given her. Queens like Emma enjoy a feeling of power and control over their environments and other, lower-status girls.

According to Wiseman, a Queen Bee is "the center of attention, and people pay homage to her." Her description of so-called Wannabes' pleasure at being "anointed" by a high school Queen Bee is strikingly similar to Harriet's first meeting with Emma. The orphan enters the novel at the side of Mrs. Goddard, who provides Emma's father with a diversion from his recurrent hypochondria. Emma watches the girl over teacups and cards and is "as much pleased with her manners as her person, and quite determined to continue the acquaintance."

Harriet is in heaven! "Miss Woodhouse was so great a personage in Highbury," that just the prospect of an introduction to her had given Harriet "as much panic as pleasure." Harriet's role in local society is precarious and can only profit from the acquaintance. After that first fateful meeting, "the humble, grateful little girl went off with highly gratified feelings, delighted with the affability with which Miss Woodhouse had treated her all the evening, and actually shaken hands with her at last!"

Emma offers Harriet the feeling that she belongs, and in return, she is, in Wiseman's words, "motivated above all else to please the person who's standing above her on the social totem pole." By hanging out with Emma, "she's in the middle of the action and has power over other girls." In return, Harriet is entirely open to Emma's charms. "Not clever," but with "a sweet, docile, grateful disposition," Harriet "was totally free from conceit, and only desiring to be guided by any one she looked up to."

At first, this adoration is highly flattering. Emma "was quite convinced of Harriet Smith's being exactly the young friend she wanted." Describing her in terms reminiscent of a decorative rug or paperweight, Harriet is declared to be "exactly the something which her home required." Tellingly, Emma herself has no illusions that her relationship with Harriet could be like that with her former governess. "Mrs. Weston was the object of a regard which had its basis in gratitude and esteem. Harriet would be loved as one to whom she could be useful."

It certainly doesn't hurt that, as Mr. Knightley remarks, Harriet "knows nothing herself, and looks upon Emma as knowing everything." Who doesn't enjoy being around someone who makes you feel brilliant and important? Emma clearly wasn't bothered by Mr. Knightley's impression that Harriet's "delightful inferiority" makes her "the very worst sort of companion that Emma could possibly have." Suitable or not, "Harriet Smith's intimacy at Hartfield was soon a settled thing."

Firmly ensconced in her idol's life, Harriet behaves just as Wiseman would expect. Devoid of personal boundaries, she is happy to do as Emma commands. While gaining a friend, she also loses herself and her own opinions.

For poet and Austen researcher Yasmine Gooneratne, Harriet's engaging nature attracts Emma. "Why? Because it soon becomes clear, her deference approximates to Emma's idea of the respect she is entitled to." Not only that, "Harriet's shyness is not inconvenient," Gooneratne proposes, as "it allows Emma to talk, and to guide the conversation of her guests as she will." Harriet shows no resistance; she doesn't push or "try to take the center of the stage, which Emma has come to regard as hers by right." Instead, Harriet Smith "is pleasantly grateful for being invited to Hartfield—her gratitude for what she clearly regards as an honor pleases and flatters Emma."

Emma justifies her condescension, deciding that "she would notice her; she would improve her; she would detach her from her bad acquaintance and introduce her into good society." As if this wasn't enough, Emma resolves that "she would form her opinions and her manners. It would be an interesting and certainly a very kind undertaking, highly becoming her own situation in life, her leisure, and powers."

Poor Harriet.

There's just one hiccup to Emma's plans. Harriet has other friends: the Martin sisters, who welcomed her into their home over the school holidays. Because they aren't part of Emma's social circle, she determines that "they must be coarse and unpolished, and very unfit to be the intimates of a girl who wanted only a little more knowledge and elegance to be quite perfect." To make matters worse, Harriet has a crush on Mr. Martin, their kindly brother.

This will not do.

In proper high school Queen Bee fashion, Emma immediately goes to work, separating Harriet from him and his family.

When Mr. Martin proposes marriage to Harriet, Emma demonstrates truly toxic egotism. Declaring to herself that the Martins were "unworthy" of Harriet, she convinces herself that unless she steps in, Harriet would be required to "sink herself forever." Yet again, Emma perceives herself as a gracious benefactor and "though very good sort of people," the Martins *must* be doing Harriet harm. Ignoring the blatantly obvious value of a match between a respected farmer and a nameless girl of questionable parentage, Emma insinuates flaws in Harriet's suitor. She questions her protégée on his reading habits, age, and appearance, warning her that Mr. Martin would be unwelcome at Hartfield—so much so that she has never even noticed him.

"I may have seen him fifty times, but without having any idea of his name," Emma proudly declares, resolving that he would be the last person on earth in whom she could be interested. Taking Harriet aside, Emma cautions her that accepting Mr. Martin would spell the end of their friendship. Emma could never have visited a Mrs. Martin; it would have been far beneath her! "I wish you may not get into a scrape, Harriet," Emma selfishly purrs. "I want to see you permanently well connected." The "idea of it" struck Harriet "forcibly . . . what an escape!" "Dear Miss Woodhouse," Harriet declares, "I would not give up the pleasure and honor of being intimate with you for anything in the world."

DON'T LOSE YOURSELF TRYING TO BELONG

Rosalind Wiseman sees behavior like Emma's on a daily basis. Two hundred years after Emma was created, Queen Bees like her continue to regulate other girls' relationships and popularity to suit their own needs. In modern high schools, these young women cause emotional rather than physical damage.

In early nineteenth-century Britain, Emma's actions could have cost a girl like Harriet much, much more. Unlike Emma, Harriet faces an uncertain and dangerous future. Once finished at Mrs. Goddard's, she will have to make her way in a harsh, misogynistic world with few employment options for women.

At best, Harriet could marry well. From Austen's description, Miss Smith doesn't have the intellectual capacity to become a governess should her marital plans fail. For girls like Harriet, life without a husband or brothers could prove bleak. Her modest education means that she could *possibly* be hired as a paid companion or chaperone. If lucky, girls like her found nice families to work for. Many weren't so fortunate; many domestics at the time faced hard lives with long working hours as well as being the frequent victims of sexual or other physical violence at the hands of their employers (or their sons).

Deborah Kaplan asserts that women in Austen's age would have known immediately that the relationship was doomed. Regency conduct books warn against intimacy between women of differing status. Historical evidence of "close, long-lasting ties between a gentlewoman and a woman beneath her in rank" like Emma and Harriet is scarce. The few known exceptions, according to Kaplan, are alliances between elite women and long-serving, senior servants such as governesses. Despite their lack of financial independence, these women were often members of the lesser gentry. These spinsters represented acceptable, educated confidantes for the wives and daughters of the affluent families who employed them.

In *Emma*, the relationship between Miss Woodhouse and her former governess, Mrs. Weston, makes perfect sense. The one between Emma and Harriet Smith decidedly *does not*. Both Mrs. Weston and Mr. Knightley agree that the orphan is "not the superior young woman which Emma's friend ought to be."

In theory, appearing in public with a higher-status girl would seem beneficial to a girl like Harriet. After all, it could increase her chances of catching a higher-status, better-settled husband. Before judging Harriet for being mercenary, it's wise to remember Robert Trivers's parental investment theory from the first chapter, arguing that competition for mates is dependent on levels of parental investment. Except for the very rich, Regency women bore most reproductive responsibility, making it incredibly important for them to find partners who could support them adequately during gestation and lactation. Biologically speaking, there is little incentive for a top-tier girl like Emma to invest in a young woman who brings nothing tangible to the relationship.

Born into wealth and comfort, Emma is entirely ignorant of the world's evils. Unlike Jane Fairfax, Harriet doesn't even have the home of an impoverished aunt to turn to when Emma inevitably becomes bored with her. As Emma herself phrases it, "a single woman, with a very narrow income, must be a ridiculous, disagreeable old maid." Reflecting on her own situation, Emma ponders that "it is poverty only which makes celibacy contemptible." "A very narrow income," Emma thinks, "has a tendency to contract the mind, and sour the temper. Those who can barely live, and who live perforce in a very small, and generally very inferior, society, may well be illiberal and cross."

With words like these, it's not a surprise that Emma's behavior toward Harriet has been the subject of harsh literary criticism ever since the book was published. Readers and critics are unsettled watching Emma encouraging Harriet to give up a farmer in hand for a parson in the bush.

Despite her protestations of affection and her family's wealth, Emma simply isn't equipped to take responsibility for Harriet's future. Literary critic Wayne Booth states, "Emma's sin against Harriet has been something far worse than the mere meddling of a busybody. To destroy Harriet's chances for happiness—chances that depend entirely on her marriage—is as close to viciousness as any author could dare to take a heroine designed to be loved."

It's this awfulness that leaves me queasy each time I read *Emma*. In *Northanger Abbey*, I can laugh at Catherine's silliness, remembering my own drama at her age. In *Sense and Sensibility*, it's fun hating Lucy

Steele and Fanny Dashwood. I'm convinced that I could never, ever treat other women as badly as they do. I love it when Aunt Norris gets her due and is banished with Maria. *Pride and Prejudice* is perfect. And *Persuasion*? I will never, ever tire of reading *that letter*.

Emma makes me question myself.

FEMALE AGGRESSION FLOWS DOWNWARD

In those painful times when I am brutally honest with myself, I know that I have been an Emma Woodhouse. While posturing about being maligned by a female boss, never having the right clothes, or being snubbed by the cheerleaders, I know that I have done the same to women who had even less than me. Like Emma, I sometimes convinced myself that it was all for the best and my motives were genuine. Still worse, I sometimes *didn't think about the consequences of my behavior at all.*

What are we supposed to do with a heroine who causes harm? What happens if the protagonist is a "con" instead of a "pro"? Emma might be able to convince herself that her treatment of Harriet is noble, but we know better.

Looking at the character through Wiseman's lens, her behavior seems typical of high school Queen Bees. These teenagers bind their Wannabes closer to themselves through matchmaking, making the most out of their romantic attachments, both good and bad. Not only do they encourage their followers to like certain boys, but they also convince them to reject others who threaten their power among their peer group.

Emma achieves this by engineering an imaginary spark between Harriet and Mr. Elton. The pursuit enhances their intimacy as a threesome. It leads to a scintillating series of orchestrated togetherness, from group sketching sessions to riddle puzzling and long walks involving shoelace sabotage.

Even Harriet's disappointment with the young curate represents a golden opportunity to become closer to Emma. Austen shares a devastatingly tragic scene of Harriet displaying her meager mementos of the imaginary romance, producing them one by one from a parcel titled *"Most precious treasures"* (italics original). Wiseman calls these "great girl bonding moments," and the silver lining of any breakup. "The intimacy that comes out of these experiences can be intense," Wiseman writes. Instead of being terrible, broken hearts are excellent opportunities for teen Queens to exert control through comforting words.

Even after watching Harriet mourn over a bit of pencil Mr. Elton discarded, she continues to lead the girl astray. Gooneratne suggests that this disturbing imbalance exposes Emma's "arrogant self-importance," usually "politely and wisely concealed when visiting neighbors in Highbury."

Like modern Wannabes, Harriet would never dream of criticizing Emma. Instead, she is ready and willing to adapt her entire life according to Miss Woodhouse's wishes. For Gooneratne, the "relationship exposes and indulges Emma's love of power, and her desire to dominate her world. Harriet is an easy victim, and in return for adoration and obedience, Emma gives Harriet her affection and her patronage."

By the time Mr. Elton brings his new bride to Highbury, Emma has groomed the vapid and biddable Harriet as her sidekick. Already having a pastime in Harriet, Emma doesn't need to befriend the curate's overbearing wife. Mrs. Elton picks up on her aversion at once, feeling "offended, probably, by the little encouragement which her proposals of intimacy met with." Shut out of Hartfield, Augusta draws back and "gradually became much more cold and distant."

Who can blame her?

There's only room for one Queen Bee in a hive, and both Emma Woodhouse and the new Mrs. Elton see themselves in the role. With Emma unavailable, Augusta seeks her own sidekick in the reluctant Jane Fairfax. Even before "a state of warfare" erupted between her and Emma, Mrs. Elton took a great fancy to the lovely and talented

Jane. To her credit, Augusta cautiously tried to team up with Emma at first. "Miss Woodhouse," she declared, "we must exert ourselves and endeavor to do something for her. We must bring her forward. Such talent as hers must not be suffered to remain unknown." Augusta underestimates Emma's inclination to keep gifted Jane well hidden.

ONE-SIDED FRIENDSHIP ISN'T FRIENDSHIP

The skewed association between Augusta and Jane parallels that of Emma and Harriet; both are unbalanced in their own way. Neither Jane nor Harriet can expect a bright, barrier-free future. Their self-appointed patronesses, Emma and Augusta, each suffer from an inflated sense of grandeur. What better way to shine than taking care of the disadvantaged, especially those who aren't dirty, diseased, or in any way displeasing? What better way for the vicar's new wife to settle in than to spend time with lonely, single girls who present no threat? By "assisting and befriending" Jane, Augusta can be reminded every day of her narrow escape from spinsterhood.

Unlike Harriet's delight at Emma's attentions, Jane has no use for the overbearing Mrs. Elton. That doesn't bother her. Ignoring the young woman's protests, Augusta persists in broadcasting Jane's dire prospects to the outside world. Ignoring the orphan's polite resistance, Augusta informs Jane of the life she should now begin living, the type of position she should seek, and which forms of work would be acceptable to her "friends." As a Queen Bee, Augusta misses the mark. She has no hold over the intelligent and accomplished Jane. Any power and gratitude Augusta hopes to receive by finding Miss Fairfax employment are nonexistent.

In her examination of minor female characters, *Women and Value in Jane Austen's Novels: Settling, Speculating, and Superfluity*, literature professor Lynda A. Hall claims that Mrs. Elton uses her attentions to Jane and her aunt "as a mark of financial superiority" and a way to build cultural capital in Highbury. Although she brought her own educational and monetary assets to the village, Mrs. Elton means to elevate herself by aiding the impoverished ladies, going so far as to call herself "Lady Patroness." This sentiment, along with her role as the vicar's wife, earn her local favor and the gratitude of local chatterbox Miss Bates.

Augusta's biggest reward for her efforts is having a legitimate, convenient excuse for avoiding her nemesis, Emma. Insisting on identifying a position of genteel servitude for her assumed protégé, Mrs. Elton whisks Jane aside for half-whispered confidences at public gatherings. Although she cannot persuade Jane to follow her guidance, her attentions allow her to dodge Emma and Harriet. Our flawed heroine watches the pair's exchanges with a sense of pity and understanding. Herself a Queen Bee, Emma immediately spots Augusta's perpetual, unwelcome assault of condescending "praise, encouragement, and offers of service."

No good can come from Emma and Augusta's misguided patronage of Highbury's distressed damsels.

Why am I so hard on Emma?

Of all of Austen's heroines, why have I singled her out the most?

It's because she has everything that (most of us) have been brought up to think that we want. She's the ideal. Not only is she pretty, but she is pampered and prosperous. Unlike the Elinors, Elizabeths, Fannys, or Catherines of the world, she has choices in life. Her family and upbringing afford her an amount of status and power, unlike her peers.

Her worst crime? Behind her beautiful clothes and proper manners, Emma is complicit in harming other women. She damages Harriet's relationships with the Martins and calls Jane's honor into question by joking around with Frank Churchill. I don't need to repeat how she disrespects poor Miss Bates.

Emma teaches us what might be the most important lesson of them all.

IF YOU DON'T KNOW WHO THE MEAN GIRL IS IN A SITUATION, IT'S PROBABLY *YOU*

In the end, Emma realizes her errors—but only after they threaten to harm her. Austen gives us delightful insight into Emma's mind as she ponders responsibility for (what she believes to be) Harriet's second broken heart. Not having learned her lesson from the Mr. Elton fiasco, Emma worries that she led the girl to fall in love with Frank Churchill. When it's revealed that he's been clandestinely engaged to Jane the whole time, Emma finally considers her actions' impact on Harriet.

At first, she "was really angry with herself," but in true Queen Bee style, the feeling rapidly subsides. She conveniently determines that she need not take all the blame. "If she could not have been angry with Frank Churchill too," Emma ponders, "it would have been dreadful." It's enough that Emma believes "she had not to charge herself, in this instance." Unlike the episode with the vicar, Emma doesn't consider herself "the sole and original author of the mischief." After all, Harriet had once mentioned that Frank was a catch.

Imagine Emma's shock when Harriet didn't mind Frank's engagement.

Suddenly, her protégée has developed a backbone. "I hope I have a better taste than to think of Mr. Frank Churchill," declares an indignant Harriet. "That you should have been so mistaken, is amazing!" she adds, confirming Emma's "great terror."

It seems that Harriet isn't interested in Frank and never has been. She's set her sights on Mr. Knightley. After months of encouragement, grooming Harriet to expect marriage above her station, Emma is rendered speechless.

Harriet's declaration of affection for Mr. Knightley awakens Emma to the folly of her behavior. Finally, "acquainted with her own heart," Emma recognizes "how improperly she had been acting by Harriet! How inconsiderate, how delicate, how irrational. How unfeeling had been her conduct!" At last, she questions herself and her motives, inwardly demanding to know "what blindness, what madness, had led her on! It struck her with dreadful force and she was ready to give it every bad name in the world."

Like so many of us, Emma only reflects on her actions once her own happiness is endangered. Not used to questioning her motives, she "was bewildered amidst the confusion of all that had rushed on her within the last few hours. . . . How to understand it all! How to understand the deceptions she had been thus practicing on herself and living under!" Emma smarts under "the blunders, the blindness of her own head and heart!" Finally, she sees herself for what she is. "With insufferable vanity had she believed herself in the secret of everybody's feelings; with unpardonable arrogance proposed to arrange everybody's destiny." In the end, "she was proved to have been universally mistaken; and she had not quite done nothing—for she had done mischief. She had brought evil on Harriet, on herself, and she too much feared, on Mr. Knightley."

WE ONLY TRULY KNOW OUR OWN EXPERIENCE

Just like I didn't know the reality of those girls back in high school, Emma is clueless (pun intended) about the lives of the women around her. At no point in the narrative does she see Harriet as anything beyond what she is—a fun accessory for Emma's outings. A pretty handbag or decorative cushion would have had as much intellectual impact as Harriet. She assumes her proper place in the narrative as "just for fun," dropped as soon as she becomes inconvenient. Emma doesn't need to genuinely interest herself in the girl's welfare because she doesn't have to. Although framed as generosity, the relationship is all about Emma and what she can get out of it, and her position in society allows it.

When Emma finally learns that "Harriet was nothing" to Mr. Knightley, all she can do for Harriet is to keep her crush a secret. "As to any of that heroism of sentiment which might have prompted her to entreat him to transfer his affection from herself to Harriet," Emma didn't have it in her. Instead, Miss Smith is gently returned to her own habitat, where she rediscovers her affection for the humble farmer who has loved her all along.

Does a tree falling in the forest make a sound if no one is around to hear it?

Is there an absolute wrong if it only takes place in fiction?

Are we complicit because we went along with Emma's misbehavior?

Austen leaves us with a warning as valid today as it was in her time. "Seldom, very seldom, does complete truth belong to any human disclosure." "Seldom," we are cautioned, "can it happen that something is not a little disguised, or a little mistaken."

I know I certainly was.

CHAPTER 6

Jane Fairfax

One Is Sick of the Very Name

Don't hate me because I'm beautiful.
—KELLY LEBROCK,
PANTENE SHAMPOO COMMERCIAL, 1986

Oh, how LeBrock's stinging words bring me back to the sticky, Aqua Net–scented days of high school. My Gen-X sisters and I racked up hundreds of hours blow-drying our hair and collecting countless first-degree curling iron burns attempting to raise our limp hair above our stations in life.

The 1980s were all about hair. The bigger, the better.

LeBrock's mane was truly aspirational, a magnificent, wavy mahogany crown ten times the size of her gorgeous face. Over-groomed and under-experienced, LeBrock's accusatory appeal struck a nerve.

It stung because it rang true. It *is* easier to hate pretty girls.

A clutch of girls at my rural high school seemed to know their own allure. Their hair was enormous. They were cute, fit, and fashionably dressed in carefully acid-damaged denim. Standing next to them in my Kmart clothes, I felt like the country mouse. I wore the same petroleum-based clearance-sale winter coat as my older brother, in sensible brown. No matter what I tried, gravity took hold of my hair. Makeup, I was told, was only for whores. Although I didn't know the meaning of the term, I knew I wanted to be one if it meant I could paint my toenails red and my eyelids blue. Back then, fitting in seemed like the most important thing in life.

In her bestselling book *Odd Girl Out: The Hidden Culture of Aggression in Girls*, Rachel Simmons takes a close look at girls considered objectionable to their peers. Quite often, the only reason is that they receive attention from boys.

The only crime worse than being attractive? *Knowing* that you were.

Those brazen hussies thought that they were "all that."

When asked to define "all that," Simmons's teenage subjects are vague and elusive. Some describe "all that" girls as wealthy, sporting fancy clothes, bragging about expensive family vacations, or living in the biggest McMansion on the cul-de-sac. For most of Simmons's subjects, "all that" boils down to one thing: popularity with boys. It doesn't seem to matter if the affection was welcome or not. An innate ability to entice hormone-crazed male classmates classifies a girl as "stuck up" and best to be avoided.

Emma is Austen's masterpiece in irrational envy. "Handsome, clever, and rich," Emma truly *is* and *has* "all that," yet has no hesitation in hindering the progress of her peer group. Simmons's concept of "all that" offers insight into Emma Woodhouse's (seemingly) inexplicable behavior, especially her aversion to Jane Fairfax. Our flawed heroine displays such a wealth of micro-aggressions that it's hard to know where to begin.

Jane's mere existence fills Emma with unreasonable resentment.

"ALL THAT" IS IN YOUR HEAD

The often-unspoken reality of adolescent girls makes it easy for readers to go along with Emma's actions toward Jane; Austen certainly primes us to. Before Jane even enters the scene, we know that Emma resents her. Spoiled, pampered Emma laments the attention Jane receives. Whining to Harriet, she grumbles that "every letter from her is read forty times over." Half-heartedly, Emma admits, "I wish Jane Fairfax very well, but she tires me to death." In an age when correspondence was the pinnacle of entertainment, Emma begrudging an old spinster and her deaf mother the joy of a few letters seems exceptionally selfish. Emma's simple, exasperated statement that she was "sick of the very name" tells me everything I needed to know.

By rights, Jane Fairfax should be the heroine of the book.

Articulate and intelligent like Jo March? Check. Orphaned and impoverished like Anne Shirley? Check. Forced to make her way in the world like Jane Eyre? Check. Reliant on the goodness of neighbors and friends to send over a few groceries now and then like Sarah Crewe? Check. Narrowly escaping a life of genteel servitude by marrying an eligible bachelor from out of town like the new Mrs. DeWinter? Check.

With all this stuff of fairy tales to back Jane up, why do readers quickly side with Emma, learning to resent the orphan's very presence?

It's because Jane Fairfax is simply too much.

She's *all that*.

The real deal (and not just because of Daddy's money, like Emma Woodhouse).

OTHER GIRLS MAY BE THREATENED BY YOU— IT'S NOT FAIR, BUT IT'S A FACT

Despite her hardships in life, Jane is worldlier than innocent bumpkin Harriet Smith and even Emma herself. She has spent significant amounts of time in the homes of wealthy friends outside of Highbury. Although underprivileged, the lovely Jane can write a fantastic letter and play the pianoforte beautifully. And yet, she's not a heroine. Like Kelly LeBrock in that old shampoo ad, the "very elegant, remarkably elegant" Jane inspires animosity just by showing up. What do we know about her? Emma's sister calls Jane sweet and amiable, as well as "very accomplished and superior." Through the delights of her aunt, we know that Jane is kind, with a tendency to send thoughtful, homemade gifts and attentions to her relatives.

Austen makes it easy for readers to reject Jane. It seems our poor little rich girl heroine is "always forced" to visit Jane when she is in Highbury. Cleverly sidestepping our suspicions, Austen's narrator allows us into Emma's mind; "why she did not like Jane Fairfax might be a difficult question to answer." We recognize her discomfort, recalling that "Mr. Knightley had once told her it was because she saw in her the really accomplished young woman, which she wanted to be thought herself." Although Emma refuted his accusation at the time, "there were moments of self-examination in which her conscience could not quite acquit her."

Somehow, her awareness lulls us into complicity.

In reality, a woman's appearance and behavior are easy targets for her peers. Most of us have probably compared ourselves to others at some point in our lives. Psychologists Steven Arnocky and Tracy Vaillancourt examine the effect of looks on female aggression in the *Oxford Handbook of Women and Competition*. Their meta-analysis of evolutionary evidence suggests (just as Austen predicted) that competition between women is significantly different from that of men. In addition to relational aggression, heterosexual women use physical attractiveness to entice suitable members of the opposite sex.

Although it may seem obvious to many, scientific investigation into the phenomenon is relatively recent. Charles Darwin's proposals on the mechanism of sexual selection inspired generations of *male* research on how *men* compete for mates. There are two basic mechanisms. The first is outright physical confrontation; the second is male display, explaining why the males of many species are more brilliantly hued than their female counterparts.

CONSIDER THE PEACOCK

Sexual selection is the only way Darwin could justify the beautiful yet physically crippling peacock's feathers. They make no physical sense. Unfurled, they render peacocks ungainly and slow, colorful targets for hungry predators. The fans themselves are irrelevant to reproduction. Evolutionary theorists believe that they signify a peacock's health and vibrance and the likelihood of his offspring's survival (if not his own). Most importantly, train-rattling (the technical term for a peacock's tail twerk) turns the ladies on. He needs them. Without a peahen, a peacock can't pass on his genetic goods.

What's not to like? Their beauty is all based on peahen choice. That's how Darwin explained the evolution of their magnificent trains over time.

Arnocky and Vaillancourt propose that a similar phenomenon occurs in humans. It's in the best interests of women considering becoming mothers to pick mates in good health and with great genes. Like peahens, studies show that women prefer men with symmetrical facial features and healthy skin. Instead of rattling their hind-feathers, men who demonstrate positive behavior have the advantage.

They find that men are also consistent in the physical characteristics they find attractive across human cultures. Like women, they prefer facial symmetry, hourglass figures, youth, and clear skin. Surprise, surprise, they're also partial to lustrous hair (like Kelly LeBrock's). It's no wonder that women are shown to invest significantly more time and money on their physical appearance than men. I probably don't need to remind you that Jane Fairfax is "very elegant, remarkably elegant," with a remarkably graceful figure and skin that "had a clearness and delicacy."

In Emma's instinctual dislike of Jane, Austen shows us something scientists are only beginning to study. It is a disheartening subject; research shows that women considered attractive tend to be victimized more often by their peers than their plain counterparts.

But wait, you say! Emma Woodhouse is considered "handsome" herself! Why should it bother her that Jane Fairfax is beautiful?

Sadly, Arnocky and Vaillancourt find that physical attractiveness plays a crucial role in female indirect aggression in *both* directions. Pretty girls aren't just more likely to *be* victims. They are also more likely to *victimize others*.

In "Tripping the Prom Queen," Vaillancourt reminds us to consider the origins of this instinct. "Intra-sexual competition may seem antiquated given the progress women in Western societies have made in recent years," Vaillancourt writes. However, "it is exceedingly unlikely that the human brain would have evolved to match this progress." After all, Vaillancourt points out, "this advancement represents less than a few decades in a trajectory of evolution that spans *millions and millions of years*" (italics original).

Today, Vaillancourt finds that 68 percent of college-age women report feeling more self-confident when in the company of a woman heavier than them. Any woman who has lost friends after weight loss can attest to this; no longer the chubby, less desirable sidekick, she often becomes redundant. "The more attractive the rival, the more threatened the competitor," Vaillancourt warns. Television viewers know that the best sidekick a heroine can have is fat and funny, like 20-teens Rebel Wilson or Melissa McCarthy (or even better, the genuinely unthreatening trifecta of fat *and* funny *and* gay). Jane Fairfax is certainly *not* that.

Despite the vast differences in their ways of life, Jane's beauty, manners, and talent represent an unwelcome element of competition for Miss Woodhouse. Emma knows very well that Jane is an infinitely more suitable companion for her than softheaded Harriet, but she turns to the weaker, less gifted girl for approval and admiration. She tells herself that Harriet is worth a hundred Jane Fairfaxes, underrating even her own intelligence in comparison "to all the charm and all the felicity" of Harriet's tender heart.

For Joyce Benenson, the reason is apparent. Lower-status girls like Harriet "will surrender all her other friendships in an attempt to form a bond with a high-status girl" like Emma Woodhouse. Despite Harriet's "charm" and "felicity," Emma recognizes deep down that the other orphan is her equal in intelligence and her superior in accomplishments.

In her envy, Emma teaches Harriet to disregard Jane, and she's only snapped out of her foolishness when Harriet's compliments verge on the ridiculous. Declaring Emma's musical abilities superior to Jane's, Emma recognizes a blatant falsehood and beseeches her companion not to class them together. Emma is forced to accept her inferiority, admitting "my playing is no more like hers than a lamp is like sunshine."

Emma Woodhouse knows that her animosity and avoidance of Jane are unfair. "It was a dislike so little just—every imputed fault was so magnified by fancy," that Emma "never saw Jane Fairfax the first time after any considerable absence, without feeling that she had injured her." Emma doesn't harass Jane directly, instead making her impoverished life difficult in stealthy ways. The most hurtful of all is her reluctance to spend time in the poor girl's presence. Instead of making friends with her intellectual equal, she chums around with unpolished Harriet Smith.

Rachel Simmons's work shows that Emma's behavior toward Jane Fairfax is well known to modern high school girls. Simmons explains that "the worst kind of silent meanness is the only one with a name: the silent treatment." Referring to it as "the most pointed kind of relational aggression," Simmons proposes that most of the time, targets don't even know why perpetrators are angry. Not only do they find themselves shut out of the girl crowd, but they also have no means to remedy the situation. Nonverbal rejection can be a potent weapon; for Simmons, "the sting of a shout pales in comparison to a day of someone's silence."

The phenomenon isn't limited to the schoolyard. Vaillancourt finds that 83 percent of female university students report intentionally ignoring a same-sex peer. Although not classified as physical aggression, these types of social exclusion have physiological as well as psychological consequences. Unlike male victims of shunning, female victims experience increased heart rates, which Vaillancourt considers an evolved response.

It doesn't escape Emma that her behavior toward Jane is disloyal. Instead of spending time with her, Emma huddles together with peacock Frank Churchill, speculating on Jane's life between visits to Highbury. Although "she doubted whether she had not transgressed the duty of woman by woman, in betraying her suspicions of Jane

Fairfax's feelings," Emma doesn't stop. She admits to herself that "it was hardly right," gossiping with Frank. Her enjoyment of his approval "made it difficult for her to be quite certain that she ought to have held her tongue."

GOSSIP IS IMPORTANT

In one aspect, Emma's resentment of Jane *is* legitimate. Miss Fairfax, it seems, fails to deal in the currency of young women—gossip. To this day, a girl's refusal to share information with her peers raises suspicion. As indicated by Rosalind Wiseman in the second chapter, gossip plays an influential role in brokering girls' relationships. As one of Wiseman's classroom subjects explains, "gossip is like money. We exchange it, sell it, and lend it out. It's what we have of value."

Jane disappoints Emma (and us readers) with rigid silence. Lacking the advantages of money, power, and status, we *should* be able to expect her to offer *at least* some entertainment in the form of news and gossip from the big, wide world. She alone has met the mysterious Frank Churchill, soon to arrive in Highbury, and refuses to describe him to Emma. Instead, she is tight-lipped and secretive.

It's not that she doesn't know what's expected. Her aunt is an open book, despite having little to say. Augusta Elton hardly stops prattling about her family home. Emma herself is full of chatter about other girls, from dissing Mrs. Elton with Harriet, speculating with Mrs. Weston, and half-listening to Miss Bates gushing over groceries.

Jane's refusal to talk about Frank is suspicious. Like Emma, we readers interpret closed-lipped Jane as a goody-two-shoes. Who does she think she is, keeping us in suspense? Austen clearly wants readers to understand the significance of Jane's omission. One chapter ends with the declaration, "Emma could not forgive her," and the next begins with it. Doubled, we are encouraged to identify with Emma.

What kind of girl refuses to talk about a single man in possession of a good fortune?

By rights, Frank Churchill should belong to Highbury. Emma should not have to depend upon Jane Fairfax for a firsthand impression of the eligible bachelor. Jane shows unforgivable reserve. Although "it was known that they were a little acquainted," the best Emma could gain from Jane were comments like "she believed he was reckoned a very fine young man," or "she believed every body found his manners pleasing." When lauded by Mr. Knightley for finally showing attention to Jane, Emma repeats her frustration. "Oh! No, I was pleased with my own perseverance in asking questions." Our heroine reports being "amused to think how little information I obtained." Emma still has no insight into Frank's looks or character despite a thorough grilling.

At this, I get mad at Jane, myself.

How dare she deny us—Emma and her devoted readers—the joy of daydreaming of a Woodhouse–Churchill wedding? Her silence prevents fantasies of flowery letters and passionate glances across crowded ballrooms. Jane's unwillingness to cooperate forestalls the expected narrative of "when Emma met Frank." We have to wait until he physically arrives in town before we can begin constructing a happy ending between him and our heroine.

Fortunately, when Mr. Churchill finally does appear, he's refreshingly willing to talk. Unlike Jane, he offers us scope for imagination. Through him, Emma and her readers can damn Jane Fairfax even more by inventing a secret rivalry between Jane and her friend Miss Campbell. We are cajoled into speculating an inappropriate relationship between her and Mr. Dixon. Galloping ahead with our conjectures, we don't stop to recognize Frank's information for what it is: a slyly planted diversion.

Emma's inappropriate scandalmongering with Frank mirrors modern gossip research. Although it often seems just idle talk, gossip transmits essential social information about romantic rivals. A frequent motif is to question a girl's integrity or virtue. By discussing the unmarried Jane with a potential suitor, Emma could seriously damage the other girl's reputation. Even worse are the covert word games she plays with Frank, insinuating a liaison between Jane and her friend's husband.

To this day, a woman's perceived sexual availability impacts how other women treat her. Along with Aanchal Sharma, Tracy Vaillancourt conducted an experiment showing that heterosexual women are intolerant of other women they perceive as reproductive threats. Subjects aged twenty to twenty-five were told that they were taking part in a study on female friendship. Randomly paired off, they were placed in a waiting room where they were interrupted by one of two women.

The interlopers pretended not to be a part of the experiment, just members of the research department retrieving equipment from the study room before the real test began. One young woman was modestly dressed in a polo shirt and khakis, with her hair up in a bun. A second was dressed provocatively, with her long hair worn loose and showing plenty of cleavage and leg. Both were the same woman; she simply changed clothing for different sets or participants.

Sharma and Vaillancourt recorded the pairs' reactions to the interloper when she left the room. Participants meeting the young woman in risqué clothing were significantly more likely to react with hostility. Some pairs didn't even wait until she left the room before slut-shaming her appearance. In a follow-up study, women who perceived another to be projecting sexual availablity reported not wanting to welcome her into their friend group.

The results were clear; physically attractive women are best avoided.

Wiseman finds similar sentiments among high schoolers. Although girl power has become a "cultural juggernaut," Wiseman contends that the widespread notion that "modesty and restraint are the essence of femininity persists." She cautions that despite feminist social advances, "our culture continues to pressure girls to be chaste." Society expects young women to be "quiet, thin, and giving." Wiseman explains that strong desires, whether for food, sex, or autonomy, are best kept silent in the girl world. The barest hint that Jane Fairfax could be less than 100 percent passive and pure encourages us to dislike her and forgive Emma for being a judgmental fool.

In retrospect, Emma knows that she has harmed Jane. How angry she must have been, watching her fiancé passing "smiles of intelligence" with another woman. Frank Churchill is (frankly) an ungainly peacock, rattling his useless but pretty train at both Emma and her readers. He postures and poses with Emma, who is conscious of the impression it makes. "In the judgment of most people looking on," Emma knows, "it must have had such an appearance as no English word but flirtation could very well describe." Austen encourages us to absolve Emma of her sins with these tiny moments of self-perception. If she isn't "quite easy" about her behavior, doesn't that mean that she is maturing?

Emma finally develops an interest in Jane after it appears that she is doomed to leave the community, pressured into servitude by the meddling Mrs. Elton. Suddenly, it becomes "a more pressing concern to shew attention to Jane Fairfax, whose prospects were closing." After ignoring the poor girl her entire life, it becomes Emma's "first wish" to show Jane kindness. We learn that "she had scarcely a stronger regret than for her past coldness." At last, "the person, whom she had been so many months neglecting, was now the very one on whom she would have lavished every distinction of regard or sympathy." Finally, when it was impossible, Emma "wanted to be of use to her." She "wanted to shew a value for her society and testify respect and consideration."

CHANNEL YOUR INNER JANE FAIRFAX

Alas, it is all too little and a little too late.

Jane Fairfax makes use of what little power she has to exit. To not engage. To walk away.

Jane isn't waiting around for Miss Woodhouse's affections. Much to Emma's surprise, the tables have been turned. Despite Emma's sudden, momentous change of heart, Jane refuses her invitation to spend a day at Hartfield. Miss Fairfax repeats the rebuff the next day, claiming to be unequal to any exercise. Arrogantly unable to believe that a poor girl could pass up spending time with her, Emma drives to the Bates's home, hoping to *force* a connection. Again, Emma is rejected.

Even more puzzling, Emma finds herself alone in being denied entrance. Both lowborn Mrs. Cole and bothersome Mrs. Elton are welcomed. Emma's sense of injustice is doubled when she learns that Jane Fairfax was spotted "wandering about the meadows, at some distance from Highbury" on the very same day "on which she had, under the plea of being unequal to any exercise, so peremptorily refused to go out with her in the carriage." At last, Emma realizes that Jane needs no kindnesses from her. Finally, herself the victim of the silent treatment, Emma "was sorry, very sorry."

It's petty of me, but I find it oddly comforting to read that even perfectly lovely characters like Jane Fairfax are unfairly rejected by their peers. While my pianoforte-playing skills are nil, Jane's experience makes me feel that my social status in school wasn't all my fault. In senior year, I had a season of bullying. Somehow, the varsity football team felt it was their duty to tell me that I was ugly. Like clockwork, one of them would whisper across the aisle what they thought of my appearance *every single day*.

No one—no girl, no boy, no teacher, nor administrator—told them to stop.

No one took me aside after class to tell me that I wasn't a hideous human being.

When I complained to the teacher, she told me that I should be flattered. Nearing retirement, she was a proponent of that old notion that if a boy was mean to you, it meant he likes you. Her attitude? I should just hold my tongue and enjoy the attention.

Somehow, her indulgent approval of their mockery was worse than their words.

How did I escape the situation? I channeled my inner Jane Fairfax. Just like Jane at Box Hill, watching the town mean girl mocking her aunt, I got up and walked away.

Hearing one hiss too many, I got up from my desk in the middle of class and went to the principal's office, where I asked for sanctuary. My refusal to return to a hostile environment didn't win me any love from the school secretary, but I finally got the teacher to notice, and the act made me feel strong.

Jane Fairfax knew the power of this, wisely making herself marvelously scarce when it suited her. Her best defense is suddenly "being ill" when Emma shows up at her door, and she prefers wandering wet meadows in lousy weather to facing Emma's "fanciful and unfair conjectures." Through Jane's absences, Emma finally learns that not everyone in town is captive to her overbearing antics.

As the Gen-X mother of a teen, I will be eternally grateful that the harassment I got in school wasn't splashed on social media, like today's victims face. Jane is safe in the pages of a novel, and I was safe in the school office. The omnipresence of social media offers little room to hide. In one incident in Russia, a group of young women beat another girl, finally forcing her to drink from a mud puddle for being "too pretty." You'd think that her humiliation was enough. No, her physical pain and degradation were magnified by a pair of bystanders who filmed the attack and uploaded it to social media. Suddenly, the whole world knew of her shame.

Such reports have become shockingly commonplace. Almost every day, it seems, some media outlet documents teenage girls being harassed by their same-sex peers. Concerned mothers share that their model daughters are relentlessly declared "ugly" by female peers on social media. Some young women go so far as to create school-wide petitions of hate against photogenic classmates. Broken down by online campaigns of gossip and harassment, young girls are tragically taking their own lives to escape.

DON'T IGNORE THE PROBLEM

Of course, I am not suggesting that women get up and flee any time things become complex (unless a woman or her children are in danger; in such cases, they should run as fast as possible—please see the appendix for resources). Jane Fairfax reminds me that choosing *not* to engage is a viable choice. There can be tremendous power in walking away or remaining silent when all you want to do is shout. If the past few political years have shown us anything, *not* rising to the occasion can be incredibly difficult. It only takes seconds for words to create irreparable wounds.

Emma finally realizes the senselessness of her jealousy toward Jane once her hidden engagement to Frank comes to light. Before, Emma displays a disturbing lack of empathy for every woman in the novel except her sister and former governess. At discovering herself deceived by both Frank and Jane, we learn that "Emma could now imagine why her own attentions had been slighted." Of course, "it had been from jealousy.—In Jane's eyes she had been a rival, and well might anything she could offer of assistance or regard be repulsed. An airing in the Hartfield carriage would have been the rack, and arrowroot from the Hartfield storeroom must have been poison." Finally, Emma "understood it all, and as far as her mind could disengage itself from the injustice and selfishness of angry feelings," she acknowledged that Jane Fairfax deserved every happiness and social advancement she received.

In his essay "Regulated Hatred," literary scholar D. W. Harding proposes that Austen's books are "read and enjoyed by precisely the sort of people she disliked." In *Emma*, Harding concludes that Austen doesn't abandon the Cinderella story entirely. Instead, she "deliberately inverts it that we ought to regard Emma as a bold variant of the theme." For Harding, Jane Fairfax is Cinderella and Emma an ugly stepsister. Like me, Harding believes that Austen deliberately encourages the mis-reading of her story, making the most of our gullibility and mistaken support for Emma Woodhouse.

OUR DISLIKE OF OTHERS SAYS MORE ABOUT US THAN IT DOES ABOUT THEM

In *Emma*, Cinderella isn't the only role Austen denies Jane Fairfax. Despite her natural beauty and elegance, her numerous accomplishments and talents, Jane isn't rewarded with a truly happy end. She is forced into uncomfortable decisions based on her financial situation, only narrowly escaping a future of servitude as a governess. Trapped by her poverty, Jane has far more in common with Charlotte Lucas than Emma Woodhouse.

Truth be told, Frank Churchill is an ass. He's only remotely more attractive as a husband than Mr. Collins because of the steady cash flow he represents. Like Collins, Frank is a man under the thumb of a domineering matriarch. Instead of Lady Catherine, he is subject to the whims of his wealthy, adoptive aunt and not at liberty to "command his own time." Until the novel's very end, the nature of Frank's inheritance rests entirely on the goodwill of a woman who could only be pleased through "a good many sacrifices."

Just like we are tricked into believing Emma Woodhouse a worthy heroine, Austen lulls readers into thinking that Frank Churchill is quite the catch. Somehow, he even manages to inspire matrimonial daydreaming in marriage-averse Emma. Even before he shows up in Highbury, readers are privileged by a glimpse into Emma's contemplation that "there was something in the name, the idea of Mr. Frank Churchill, which always interested her." She muses that Frank "was the very person to suit her in age, character, and condition" if she were ever to tie the knot.

Regardless of his status as a single man in possession of a good fortune, Frank exhibits a wanton lack of character. Undeniably inconsistent, he doesn't show up to his father's wedding and takes his time visiting the newlyweds. Using his aunt as an excuse, he placates them with "fine flourishing letter[s], full of professions and falsehoods."

Mr. Knightley was right, believing Frank's letters were tools to "persuade himself that he has hit upon the very best method in the world of preserving peace at home and preventing his father's having any right to complain."

Even worse, Frank actively leads Emma on, shamelessly and cruelly gossiping and flirting with her in front of his intended. Using "fine words" and "hyperbolical compliments," he exchanges "smiles of intelligence" with Emma, poking fun at Jane's appearance from across the room. Like Charlotte Lucas, poor Jane is faced with two unpleasant decisions: either face an uncertain future or marry an idiot.

Eyes wide open, she chooses the latter, and it's not our place to judge her for it. Despite all her beauty, Jane Fairfax marries a beast, and one unlikely to transform into an honest, respectful prince. We can only hope that, like Mr. Collins, Frank enjoys spending time in his garden.

Part III

AUSTEN'S PROTO-KARENS

Where There Is a Disposition to Dislike,
a Motive Will Never Be Wanting

CHAPTER 7

Lady Susan

The Females of the Family Are United Against Me

There was a little girl who had a little curl
right in the middle of her forehead and when
she was good she was criticized anyway.

—ELAN GOLOMB

Until now, it's been relatively easy to blame Austen's mean girls on youth and inexperience. Science tells us that the prefrontal cortex, the part of the brain responsible for decision making and moderating social behavior, isn't fully developed until sometime in our mid-twenties. That means that characters like Lucy Steele, Isabella Thorpe, and even our beloved Elizabeth Bennet are only on the verge of maturity. It will take them another few years to suppress their urges and realize the consequences of their behavior. Until then, they can have a hard time telling right from wrong.

Fortunately (or unfortunately), humans need a fully developed prefrontal cortex to feel guilt or remorse, explaining how easy it is for Austen's mean girls to gloss over their misdeeds (and why I'm known to softly mutter "prefrontal cortex, prefrontal cortex, prefrontal cortex" to myself when frustrated by my teenager's behavior—it helps).

Distracted by Austen's delightfully antiquated writing, it's easy to forget her heroines' extreme youth. When they were written, her main characters were considered old enough to marry and begin bearing enormous numbers of children. Today, kids that age aren't regarded as mature enough to even rent cars in their own name (I'm looking at you, carriage joyrider John Thorpe!).

Austen's spiteful adults are harder to forgive. Not only *should* their brains be fully developed, the Lady Susans, Fanny Dashwoods, and Lady Catherine de Bourghs of the world have found husbands and started families. The source of their hostility is no longer attracting a man but retaining personal autonomy.

What is the scarcity driving their awfulness? It's doubtful women like them ever knew hunger or real hardship, despite being subjected to profoundly pervasive misogyny their entire lives. And yet, Austen's adult antagonists appear threatened by young protagonist women representing no significant challenge to them or their livelihoods.

So why do they leverage their advantages for evil instead of good?

MEAN GIRLS CAN BECOME MEAN MOMS

Mothers misbehave particularly badly in Austen's work. Instead of providing comfort and affection, they are, at best, disinterested, and at worst, genuinely monstrous. There are no nurturing and selfless Marmies or Mrs. Weasleys in sight.

Granted, our modern expectations of motherhood differ drastically from what Austen would have known. Until fairly recently, married motherhood was considered a woman's key objective in life. Until the advent of birth control and fertility treatments, pregnancy was determined by nature alone. Austen would have certainly recognized making babies a woman's main priority was problematic; childbirth cost the lives of three of her sisters-in-law. Having babies was the most common cause of death for Regency women, and two in ten women and infants didn't make it through alive. Those who survived pregnancy relied on their families for financial support, and any mother or child unlucky enough to lack male relatives was on her own.

As a mother myself, it's hard to imagine the psychological impact of knowing that your own and your baby's chances of survival were iffy at best. Children born in the Regency had roughly a one-in-three chance of making it past their fifth birthday. That knowledge clearly didn't turn Jane Austen's mother, the former Cassandra Leigh, into an overprotective helicopter parent. Of her brood of eight, she fostered out one who wasn't considered to be developing typically and allowed another to be adopted by wealthy cousins.

Reading between the lines of Austen's remaining letters, her mother seems to have been a bit of a hypochondriac. Like anxious Mrs. Bennet or languid Lady Bertram, Mrs. Austen "suffered" often. Remarkably, despite her frequent ailments requiring laudanum and leeches, Cassandra Leigh Austen made it to the ripe old age of eighty-seven. Sadly, her youngest daughter, our beloved Jane, only made it to forty-one.

We'll never be sure of her inspiration, but Austen's early epistolary novella, *Lady Susan*, outlines the first of her manipulative matriarchs. Describing its incredibly narcissistic, shape-shifting title character, it seems Austen had intimate knowledge of selfish mother figures. Penned around the time she was twenty, Austen never sought publication for the narrative, a clever move for someone who may have been struggling under a narcissistic parent herself.

In *Lady Susan*, Austen chronicles the not-very-motherly escapades of the newly widowed Lady Susan Vernon. It's structured in two sets of letters, exchanged in parallel. The first is from Lady Susan herself, writing to her brother-in-law, followed by correspondence with her friend, Mrs. Alicia Johnson. The second set is posted among the family of Charles Vernon's wife, the De Courcys. Readers quickly clue into the disconnect between appearances and reality; Lady Susan will stop at nothing to get her own way.

BE WARY OF ISSUING OFFHAND INVITATIONS

We meet the "excessively pretty" widow in her letter to Charles Vernon, inviting herself to stay at Churchill, his estate. Being a nice guy, he made a perfunctory remark at his brother's funeral, telling Lady Susan that she would always be welcome in his home. It's clear he never dreamed she would take him up on it so quickly and that he also failed to inform his wife, Catherine. She was *not* amused; after all, Lady Susan actively opposed her marriage to Charles and made sure they didn't have the opportunity to buy Vernon Castle when it was forced to be sold.

The titular character knows what's expected of her as a houseguest and widowed mother. She peppers the declaration of her impending visit with hyperbolic professions of anticipated delight at finally meeting Charles's wife and "dear little children." Her intention to stay is definite; there is no way Charles can misunderstand (or decline) her self-invitation, which ends with the ominous assurance, "I am determined, you see, not to be denied admittance."

In contrast to this gushing letter to Charles, Lady Susan gripes to her friend Alicia that the move is a "last resource," adding, "were there another place in England open to me I would prefer it." The reality is, Lady Susan behaved so badly at the last place she stayed that she needs to remain with the Vernons until finding "something better in view."

She arrives at Churchill after a disastrous stint with the Mainwarings of Langford, where she flirted shamelessly with her host, driving his wife to distraction. Not satisfied with one conquest, she seduces a second houseguest, the "contemptibly weak" Sir James Martin, "a young man engaged to Miss Mainwaring." Writing to Alicia, Susan bewails, "the females of the family are united against me." It was time "to be gone." When she finally leaves the scene of her crimes, "the whole party was at war"; Mrs. Mainwaring was "insupportably jealous" and her daughter "highly incensed."

Lady Susan is just annoyed at having to move; their pain doesn't affect her.

Despite the Mainwaring ladies' fury and rage, Lady Susan admits no wrong, resenting their behavior instead. She won't acknowledge that making Sir James "distractedly in love with her" was a shitty thing to do, calling it a victory instead. She justifies her actions as the "sacred impulse of maternal affection," announcing to Alicia that the absurdly stupid man is just the guy for her sixteen-year-old daughter, Frederica.

Readers aren't hoodwinked for long. In the very next line, she describes Frederica as "the torment of my life" and "the greatest simpleton on earth."

How motherly.

Not only is Lady Susan a narcissistic, grown-up mean girl, she's a *bad mom*.

NOT ALL BAD MOMS ARE ADORABLY EXHAUSTED #WINEMOMS

Gentle readers, please don't confuse Lady Susan's terrible actions with those of twenty-first-century #BadMoms. Hollywood would have us believe that the suburbs are overrun with packs of day-drinking, PTA-defying #BadMoms. They cruise the cul-de-sacs in their crumb-dusted, empty-juice-box-filled minivans, finding release in occasional Merlot binges and boisterous girls' nights out.

Raucous, modestly raunchy #BadMoms are lucrative. Any number of alcohol and angst-soaked films, from *Moms' Night Out* (2014), *Bad Moms* (2016), *A Bad Moms Christmas* (2017), and *Fun Mom Dinner* (2017), depict overextended mothers living in McMansions filled with loopy-lettered signs reading "wine a little, laugh a lot," "sip happens," and "it's wine o'clock."

Nope.

Lady Susan is not a harmless hashtag. The difference between #BadMoms and Austen's evil mother? These tender-hearted, affectionate creatures love their children fiercely. No matter where they land on the sobriety scale, Western popular culture's #BadMoms transform into ferocious mama bears at the merest whiff of danger toward their sprouts. I bet most moms, hashtag or not, feel the same.

Now that I have been a parent for almost two decades, criticizing other women's mothering skills feels like walking a tightrope, without a net, in a hurricane. Those of you who have ever been pregnant will know what I mean. Just *thinking* about having a child opens you up for criticism. It seems that *everyone* has an opinion on what mothers should do and be. Society's expectations of moms, whether biological, adopted, step, or foster, feel so unreasonably high that it feels like a betrayal to attack even a fictional one.

Perfect mothers do not exist. There, I've said it. Nevertheless, many of my fellow moms and I have felt immense pressure to be the angelic, all-giving, all-knowing, selfless mothers the media celebrates. These notions simply don't—*can't*—match up with reality. As for me, becoming a mom was astonishingly emotional, a perfect storm of overwhelming, unconditional love crashing against incredible self-doubt. Even after forty weeks of gestation, it felt unbelievable that I had made a human being and that the world trusted me with him. Parenthood (and for some, the aching desire for it) can make us raw and vulnerable in previously unimaginable ways.

I approached motherhood the way I knew best—by obsessively reading anything I could get my hands on. It could have been the hormones or the painkillers from the unplanned cesarean, but my insecurities were at an all-time high by the time my son was born. Every decision took on a new significance. Despite my theoretical knowledge, I worried about the perfect little being I had brought into the world. Had that glass of celebratory bubbly before my positive pregnancy test harmed him? Had my second trimester craving for additive-packed sugar cereal doomed him to struggle in the world? The doubts piled on as I rationalized the proper ratio of playdates to business meetings or screen time and my own desperate need to take a shower.

However imperfect we appear, most of us do our best for our kids in a world full of different "expert" opinions. We take folic acid and avoid sushi, thoughtfully commit to a feeding style right for us and our infants, and carefully weigh the value of staying at home against needing regular income. Whatever we choose leaves us open for criticism; blaming mothers is a cultural punchline. Of course, it's our fault! Of course, they will need therapy!

While others chuckle, we secretly hope that it won't happen to *ours*.

Facing facts, not all moms are suited (or even interested) in the vocation. Motherhood can be *damn hard*, and not everyone is wired for it. Child abuse at the hands of parents is shocking and often results from them having been maltreated themselves. That's an explanation, *not* an excuse. Not all women have the emotional capacity for the role, and not all have a choice in it. I won't go into the darkest depths of family betrayal I have learned about in my friends' lives but want readers who have struggled under harmful parents to know that *you are seen* (and I desperately hope that you have been able to distance yourself and heal).

BEAUTIFUL BONNETS CAN HIDE HORNS

Despite still-pervasive Victorian notions of angelic mothers, the world has consistently recognized that not all of them are nurturing. There's the Old Testament woman who would rather see a baby chopped in half than share it with another. Euripides' Medea murders her children because her husband leaves her for a rival. Finding her baby Hephaestus deformed, Hera throws him off a mountain. Shakespeare's awful mom, Tamora in *Titus Andronicus*, dishes up her children baked in a pie. If a Grimm brother had written *Lady Susan*, Frederica would have been dropped off at the forest edge, left to be shot by a huntsman or eaten by a gingerbread-housed witch.

Frederica Vernon is one of literature's unwanted daughters. She is an inconvenient, lingering reminder and responsibility from her mother's late marriage. Instead of filling the girl up with poisoned apples, Lady Susan uses her to create fiction within fiction. She knows what society expects of her and takes great pains to appear accordingly. Her physical loveliness aids her hoax. Catherine Vernon is surprised to find her "delicately fair, with fine grey eyes and dark eyelashes," assuming a "gentle, frank, and even affectionate" manner of speaking. Knowing that the key to Catherine's (healthy, maternal) heart is "through the children," Lady Susan memorizes their names in advance. Her emotions are regulated and pre-planned, she strategizes attaching herself "with the greatest sensibility to one, in particular, a young Frederic, whom I take on my lap and sigh over."

No one could win Lady Susan's affection through Frederica, although she takes great pains to convince those around her otherwise. Her newest conquest, Catherine's unsuspecting brother Reginald, believes Lady Susan to be an "unexceptionable" mother. His gullibility delights Lady Vernon, who is proud that her manipulative skills have hit their mark. "I never behaved less like a coquette in the whole course of my life," she crows in a letter to Alicia, adding, "though perhaps my desire of dominion was never more decided." She subdues Reginald De Courcy "entirely by sentiment and serious conversation." Without "the semblance of the most commonplace flirtation," she exults, she is able to make him "at least half in love with me." She uses the same tactics to convince him that instead of abandoning her daughter at boarding school, she placed her altruistically "in hands where her education will be properly attended to." In contrast, Lady Susan calls Frederica "a chit, a child, without talent or education" to her friend.

The De Courcy women are harder to convince. Prepared for Lady Susan's machinations, Catherine Vernon describes her unwanted guest as a "mistress of deceit" in a letter to her mother. Reflecting on the mismatch between the widow's reputation and appearance, she writes that "if I had not known how much she has always disliked me for marrying Mr. Vernon . . . I should have imagined her an attached friend." Catherine admits, "she has already almost persuaded me of her being warmly attached to her daughter, though I have been so long convinced to the contrary."

Lady Susan spreads lies about Frederica at any opportunity, telling her in-laws that the girl was the unfortunate victim of an imperfect governess. Although she speaks of her daughter with "tenderness and anxiety," Catherine Vernon distinctly remembers Lady Susan frequently abandoning Frederica in the countryside while she frolicked and flirted her way through London. When Frederica, followed by Sir James, shows up at Churchill, Catherine can observe the noxious mother–daughter relationship firsthand.

NOT ALL MOTHERS ARE MATERNAL

Writing to her mother, Catherine observes that Frederica remains silent when Lady Susan is around, yet "talks enough when alone with me to make it clear that if properly treated . . . she would always appear to much greater advantage." Slowly but surely, Catherine wins her niece's trust, finding a "peculiar sweetness in her look when she speaks either to her uncle or me, for as we behave kindly to her we have of course engaged her gratitude." "We are very good friends," she concludes, remarking that Lady Susan clearly has "no real love" or affection for the girl.

The attachment incenses Lady Susan. Not only does she resolve to punish her daughter "pretty severely," but also Reginald and Catherine for receiving Frederica "so favorably." In a letter to Alicia she exults, "I must torment my sister-in-law for the insolent triumph of her look and manner," elaborating that "there is exquisite pleasure in subduing an insolent spirit," who is "predetermined to dislike one's superiority." Lady Susan obviously views her visit to Churchill as sport, declaring "it should be my endeavor to humble the pride of these self-important De Courcys still lower." The "project will serve at least to amuse me," she boasts.

Unlike Catherine and Charles, Lady Susan doesn't recognize Frederica as a person. Instead, she treats her daughter as an extension of herself, a pawn. The widow is indignant when anything deviates from her plan and is only interested in her child when it suits her purposes. Lady Susan constantly criticizes Frederica, referring to her as "stupid"; having "nothing to recommend her"; a "tiresome," "horrid" encumbrance. The young widow is quick to anger, demanding complete compliance with her commands. She relies on her daughter's fear to maintain a pretense of goodness. "Frederica is too shy, I think, and too much in awe of me to tell tales," Susan triumphs to Alicia, adding, "but if the mildness of her uncle should get anything out of her, I am not afraid. I trust I shall be able to make my story as good as hers."

Sadly, there is truth in Frederica. Growing up with an emotionally abusive mother like Lady Susan can be debilitating. The youthful antics of Lucy Steele and Caroline Bingley pale in comparison to the damage Lady Susan inflicts on the women around her, but most importantly on her own child.

Austen's depiction of Lady Susan aligns with what modern psychologists term "narcissistic personality disorder" (NPD). You may remember the story of Narcissus from Greek mythology. Narcissus was the son of a river god and a nymph. He was a beautiful boy who fell in love with himself after seeing his reflection in a pool of water. There are various stories of his ultimate demise, either wasting away, unable to wrest himself away from his own image, or falling into the water and drowning. Whatever the ending, the story of Narcissus is a morality tale, cautioning against vanity and self-involvement.

YOU CAN'T ARGUE WITH A NARCISSIST

The fifth edition of the American Psychiatric Association's *Diagnostic and Statistical Manual of Mental Disorders* classifies NPD as a category B personality disorder. In simple terms, adults with NPD tend to believe that they are better, smarter, and more attractive than the rest of the population. Convinced they are the center of the universe, they are resentful when others don't afford them the admiration they think they deserve. NPD is a spectrum disorder, ranging from nonclinical self-centeredness to the full-blown disorder.

Most of us have likely encountered someone like Austen's wicked widow. Experts estimate that 1–2 percent of the US population shows signs of narcissistic personality disorder like Lady Susan, leading to long-term suffering and even PTSD for those around them. Austen certainly knew *at least* one by the time she was twenty, to describe the symptomatic behaviors so accurately. Her gift to readers is a way to witness NPD from the safe distance of paragraphs and pages.

On the surface, Lady Susan's behavior may seem hyperbolic, but an exaggerated sense of self-importance is one of the disorder's key signifiers. The widow's favorite topic in every letter is herself. Even when mentioning others, it's only in reference to her own needs. She demonstrates an excessive craving for admiration, and is convinced of her own beauty, eloquence, and charm. It's not hard to imagine her modern equivalent, dedicating her life to social media, sharing the minutia of her days, driven by "likes," and convinced of the world's interest in pictures of her every move and meal.

The strikingly lovely widow has no qualms exploiting others for her own purposes. It never occurs to her that her self-invitation to Churchill could be inconvenient, when her arrival prevents the Vernons from spending Christmas with Catherine's mother as planned. She is inexplicably surprised at Catherine's lukewarm welcome. "I wanted her to be delighted at seeing me," she complains in a letter to Alicia. "I was as amiable as possible on the occasion, but all in vain. She does not like me. To be sure when we consider that I DID take some pains to prevent my brother-in-law's marrying her, this want of cordiality is not very surprising, and yet it shews an illiberal and vindictive spirit to resent a project which influenced me six years ago, and which never succeeded at last."

Lady Susan lacks empathy for anyone, from her own daughter to the Mainwaring ladies and the entire De Courcy clan. She doesn't hesitate to take advantage of others wherever she can; in one letter she calls her brother-in-law "insipid," delighting in another that "he is so easily imposed upon!" Of her actions to Reginald, she claims indifference, as she "infinitely" prefers "the tender and liberal spirit of Mainwaring, which, impressed with the deepest conviction of my merit, is satisfied that whatever I do must be right."

Narcissist Lady Susan believes that she is exceptional, punishing anyone who fails to realize it. Commenting on Catherine's brother to Alicia, she gloats, "there is something about him which rather interests me, a sort of sauciness and familiarity which I will teach him to correct."

Knowing he has been prejudiced by his sister, the widow discloses "there is exquisite pleasure in subduing an insolent spirit, in making a person predetermined to dislike acknowledge one's superiority."

IT'S ALL ABOUT MOM

Of all her victims, Lady Susan hurts her daughter the most. While other adults have options for escaping Susan's scrutiny, Frederica has only one mother. Lady Susan has no interest in the sixteen-year-old. Her goal? Frederica's marriage to affluent idiot Sir James. The match might make fiscal sense, but the notion of forced marriage is alarming.

Lady Susan switches tactics when her command misfires. "Upon the whole, I commend my own conduct in this affair extremely," Lady Susan writes, indicating that her demands are "a very happy instance of circumspection and tenderness." While she claims that "some mothers would have insisted on their daughter's accepting so good an offer on the first overture," Lady Susan boasts that she will use stealth instead. Instead of forcing Frederica "into a marriage from which her heart revolted," she plans to "make it her own choice, by rendering her thoroughly uncomfortable till she does accept him." Susan's letter to Alicia leaves no doubt; Frederica "shall have him." After all, her mother does "not by any means want to be" by her side. Clearly strained by reporting about someone besides herself, Lady Susan quickly changes subjects with an abrupt "enough of this tiresome girl."

In *Will I Ever Be Good Enough? Healing the Daughters of Narcissistic Mothers*, psychotherapist Dr. Karyl McBride explores the gendered dynamic of maternal narcissism. Herself the daughter of a narcissist, she posits that while both boys and girls suffer, the ramifications are different depending on the dyad involved: father–son, father–daughter, mother–son, or mother–daughter. "A mother," McBride explains, "is her daughter's primary role model for developing as an individual, lover, wife, mother, and friend." As a result, "aspects of maternal narcissism tend to damage daughters in particularly insidious ways."

Girls growing up with emotionally absent caregivers like Lady Susan often reach adulthood looking for affection from anyone willing to give it. Not having known unconditional love and empathy, these girls lack true emotional connection. "In severe cases of maternal narcissism, where neglect or abuse is involved, the most basic level of parental care is missing," McBride relates. It can be extremely confusing for girls who see the nurturing their friends and relatives receive, making them wonder if they are somehow lacking or to blame. They grow up anxious of separation and abandonment, feelings that can last throughout their lives.

Lady Susan can't believe that anyone could love Frederica for herself. She explains Catherine's interest in the girl as an ego booster. "She is exactly the companion for Mrs. Vernon," Susan decides, as Mrs. Vernon "dearly loves to be firm and to have all the sense and all the wit of the conversation to herself."

Pot, let me introduce you to my friend Kettle.

SOMETIMES THE BEST MOTHER FOR YOU ISN'T YOUR OWN

Lady Susan ends abruptly. "To the great detriment of the Post Office revenue," the unnamed narrator relates wryly. In its brief conclusion, Lady Susan slyly relinquishes her daughter to the De Courcys, sneaking off to marry silly Sir James herself. She loses her only female friend, as Alicia's husband is so disgusted by Lady Susan's behavior that he threatens his wife's banishment should the relationship continue.

The one good action Lady Susan commits is an inaction. After a few perfunctory, artful letters, we learn that she "ceased to write" to Frederica. Her silence is a blessing; experts on coping with narcissistic parents advise to limit contact with their abuser if all else fails. Since narcissistic trauma is often transferred from generation to generation, separation combined with therapy may be the only way to stop the cycle.

According to McBride, "If a girl is fortunate, she may find another adult who can help her, recognize and validate her feelings and provide some measure of guidance." Once safely ensconced at Churchill, the end of Frederica's relationship with her birth mother makes room for new, trusting, healthy relationships with her aunt and uncle. She represents a growing wave of individuals who establish their own support systems after escaping their childhood homes. Unlike Lady Susan, Frederica enjoys the happiest of possible endings the child of narcissistic parents can have—she redefines family on her own.

"Chosen families" can be a source of strength and affirmation for those rejected by their birth families, especially in LGBTQ+ circles. Sadly, a 2017 study published in *Pediatric Clinics of North America* claims that one third of gay, lesbian, and bisexual youth are rejected by their parents for their sexual orientation. Fortunately for Frederica Vernon, she is finally *seen* and accepted by her aunt. "My heart aches for her," Catherine writes to her mother. Finally free, Frederica goes on to enjoy a historically appropriate (yet nevertheless icky) marriage to her uncle-in-law, Reginald De Courcy, who only had to be "talked, flattered, and finessed into an affection for her."

FOR THE CHILDREN OF NARCISSISTS, RECOGNITION HELPS

Lady Susan Vernon is a terrible person, but she is the only mother that Frederica has. I've known women with narcissistic mothers who spend decades trying desperately to win their mothers' approval through excelling at academics or starving themselves to fit their mother's critical eye. Sadly, McBride explains, these women need to come to terms with the fact that their mothers will never change. "Most narcissists lack the capacity to give significant, authentic love and empathy," she counsels. Sadly, their children have no choice but to "deal with this reality." "Accepting that your own mother has this limited capacity is the first step," McBride suggests. "Let go of the expectation that it will ever be different."

McBride encourages her patients to work through three steps to recover. First, they need to recognize the problem and to understand that their experience was not healthy, and to examine its origins. The second, harder step for daughters raised without recognition or validation of their feelings, is to process their experiences. Lastly, girls like Frederica must learn to separate themselves from their mothers, allowing time to grieve for the relationship that never was.

The question remains: if Lady Susan is so awful, why do we love reading about women like her?

English professor and theorist Ellen Spolsky suggests that experiencing the Lady Susans and Fredericas of the world through stories is a form of "nourishment." By representing lifelike characters (however hyperbolic) with whom we can identify, individuals and communities can confront their demons from a distance. Living vicariously through them, we are safely exposed to a wide variety of people and predicaments. It's no wonder book sales skyrocketed during the COVID-19 lockdown. While some stories may be painful, studies show that reading about fictional characters going through difficulties like our own can be exceptionally comforting.

The best part? We don't even need to leave the house, and we can always expect a happy ending.

CHAPTER 8

Fanny Dashwood Did Not at All Approve

To feel envy is human. To savor Schadenfreude is devilish.
—ARTHUR SCHOPENHAUER

It's easy to spot privilege in a Jane Austen novel. Within just a few paragraphs, we know the lay of the land, who has money and who doesn't. In her pre-industrial world, privilege belonged primarily to men, defined according to strict hierarchies based on bloodlines, fortune, and vocation. What little agency women had corresponded to that of the men in their lives, but in miniature. Readers quickly learn which young women face a hard road ahead, which must be grateful for any opportunity, and which are entitled to have a mind of their own.

Austen's first published novel, *Sense and Sensibility*, lays the framework for a literary career describing female betrayal under the guise of romance. Through a minor character, Fanny Dashwood, Austen shows us the brutal sting of family disloyalty and the flimsiness of promises made. At its core, it's a novel of female power: power had, power used, power lacked, and power grabbed.

Arguably Austen's most evil creation, Fanny manipulates the men in her life, often bending them to her will. Austen doesn't tell us much about Mrs. John Dashwood, other than that she's privileged. Like most married women of her age, Fanny wields no social authority and is dependent on her equally "cold-hearted" husband. As soon as they wed, any dowry she brought into their union legally became his. This lack of financial agency doesn't stop her from making the most of her situation. Together with her arrogant and advantaged mother, she's determined to dictate what happens to her husband's fortune, holding the purse strings as tightly closed as possible.

DON'T BE A FANNY[1]

We meet Fanny after the death of her father-in-law, who begged his only son to provide for his second family after his passing. The nature of the Dashwood estate excludes the three daughters from his second marriage from inheriting anything beyond a modest sum. John, who was "amply provided for by the fortune of his mother" as well as his own lucrative marriage, swears to comply, allowing his father to die in peace.

Old Mr. Dashwood isn't cold in his grave before John's "narrow-minded and selfish wife," Fanny, begins a campaign to negate his vow. John initially intends to be generous; after all, he and his wife have enough cash. Mercenary Fanny categorically "did not at all approve" of this ambition. Her manner of attack? She deflects attention from the matter at hand. Instead of displaying compassion to the Dashwood ladies, Fanny challenges her husband to think of "their poor little Harry," claiming that "it was well known that no affection was ever supposed to exist between the children of any man by different marriages."

Her tactics are varied. With startling self-assurance based on nothing, Fanny tells her husband that he will "ruin himself" by helping his half-sisters too much. When this fails, she questions the soundness of his father's mind when making his last request. "He did not know

---

1. For those who may be concerned, yes, I am aware that the term "fanny" in modern British English refers to the same reproductive lady part as the "C" word, which many of us Americans are too prudish to use. Who knows, maybe Austen inspired the connotation, seeing as Fanny Dashwood is *definitely* a "C."

what he was talking of, I dare say." Shameless, Fanny continues: "Ten to one, but he was light-headed at the time. Had he been in his right senses, he could not have thought of such a thing as begging you to give away half your fortune from your own child."

Fanny escalates, demanding, "How could he answer it to himself to rob his child" by distributing his inheritance equitably? Over and over, Fanny reinforces the kinship argument. "What possible claim could the Miss Dashwoods have, who were related to him only by half-blood? . . . What brother on earth would do half so much for his sisters, even if really his sisters!" she appeals. Her words are hyperbolic, even violent. Fulfilling his vow would mean "impoverishing" their child, she implores.

In normal circumstances, I'd applaud a woman making the most of her financial resources, celebrating her strong leadership skills and psychological insight. After all, Fanny has managed to make the lemon of Regency womanhood as palatable for herself as possible.

So, what's my problem?

Fanny's lemonade-making damages the women around her.

DON'T SOUR OTHER WOMEN'S LIVES
TO SWEETEN YOUR OWN

At the beginning of the nineteenth century, it was common knowledge that a father's death could mean poverty for his survivors. Many widows and children became instant charity cases. You only need look at a single issue of *The Bath Chronicle* to get an idea of their desperation. Take "The Melancholy Situation of Widow Tabor." After her husband the hosier was run over by a wagon three (!) times, Mrs. Tabor was left with "not a bed to lie on, nor a sixpence to support herself and her two children." A once proud tradesman's wife, she was thankful for "the smallest donations." Her plight shares the page with that of former schoolmarm Mary Rogers. "A Person in Great Distress," Mary suffered from a "rheumatic complaint without hopes of a cure," and could no longer keep herself. Between instructions on potato farming and an ad for nipple cream, the third page tells the story of Daniel Sheppard's death by drowning and the wife and five children he left behind. "The eldest (13) blind in one eye and much afflicted, the youngest three years old and afflicted with fits," the "smallest donations will be gratefully received and acknowledged." Yet another article relates the fate of a publican's daughter who eloped with a soldier from Ireland; left "nearly naked and penniless," she only survived after being saved by the Chief Magistrate, who sent the girl to an infirmary—funded by charitable concerts like the one advertised on the previous page.

Charity toward the Dashwood ladies is the last thing on Fanny's mind. Instead, she resembles a phenomenon currently festering in Western society: Karen. Fanny is an entirely average white woman who feels inexplicably entitled to dictate the lives of others. You'll know her from social media. Almost daily, the actions of a new, so-called Karen flood our screens. Inevitably, her behavior appears to stem from an overinflated sense of entitlement: a perceived right to ignore leash mandates at the dog park, a belief that only "certain kinds of people" should have to wear masks, enjoy public spaces, or be allowed to wait for friends at Starbucks. The origin of the pejorative is unclear. Neither *Wikipedia* nor *Urban Dictionary* is much help.

Whatever the basis, the message is clear; so-called Karens, like Fanny, are interested only in themselves.

FORGET "EVERYTHING NICE"

Fanny (and Karen) goes against centuries of female conditioning. In their book, *Feminist Nightmares: Women at Odds: Feminism and the Problems of Sisterhood*, Susan Ostrov Weisser and Jennifer Fleischner explain that male hostility and aggression are so ubiquitous that they are expected rather than surprising. We learn to ignore it.

If I had a dime for every time a guy man-spread me out of a subway seat, stole my ideas at work, or told me to smile, I could afford a private jet to fly away from their nonsense. Instead, I've learned to keep quiet. Brushing it off is often the only realistic way to prevent mansplaining about "overdramatic" and "militant" feminism for simply being myself.

Weisser and Fleischner posit that we learn to expect more of women from an early age, recognizing that they are the world's caretakers. When our peers fail to live up to our assumptions, Weisser and Fleischner explain, our disappointment and anger are "more acute because we are less armored against it." It's harder to forget aggression from other women; it goes straight to the bone.

SISTERLY LOVE ISN'T A GIVEN

There's no love lost between Fanny and her in-laws; "Mrs. John Dashwood had never been a favorite." The sentiment didn't go unnoticed. Immediately after the funeral, "Mrs. John Dashwood, without sending any notice of her intention to her mother-in-law, arrived with her child and their attendants." She installs herself as the lady of the house without hesitation, degrading the Dashwood ladies to "the condition of visitors" in their own home.

Norland Park quickly becomes a hostile environment, much to Fanny's delight. She "had had no opportunity, till the present, of shewing" the Dashwoods "how little attention to the comfort of other people she could act when occasion required it." Although Fanny has every right to live at Norland, basic decorum would have slowed her rush. Her lack of compassion is apparent; finally, she has power over the women who had ignored her. She intends to rule the household immediately, becoming the matriarch of the neighborhood.

Fanny works hard to implement and keep control. Suspecting a blossoming romance between her awkward eldest brother, Edward, and Miss Dashwood, she does her best to nip it in the bud. She and her mother have no intention of letting Edward pick his bride; together, they have determined that he is to marry rich.

CHAPTER 8

LISTEN TO YOUR HEART, NOT YOUR FANNY[2]

Elinor and Edward aren't interested in her opinion. Their obvious attachment soon begins to make Fanny "uneasy, and at the same time, (which was still more common), to make her uncivil." Fanny asserts her perceived right of veto, using the Regency equivalent of calling the manager: badmouthing Elinor to her mother. Fanny's primary weapon is her words, warning the elder Mrs. Dashwood that Edward has "great expectations" and that "any young woman who attempted to draw him in" would not be treated kindly.

Accusing Elinor of being a scheming predator hits its mark. After months lingering in her former home, Mrs. Dashwood finally wakes up, resolving to depart immediately so that "her beloved Elinor should not be exposed another week to such insinuations." There is only room for one Queen at Norland Park.

It's (unsurprisingly) easy to forgive spineless John Dashwood for screwing over his half-sisters. After all, it was all his wife's idea.

SOME RELATIVES ARE BEST ENJOYED FROM A DISTANCE

Even the Dashwood women's removal to the safety of a modest cottage in Devonshire incites Fanny's ire. Instead of being satisfied at finally having the house to herself, she resents the women taking the "household linen, plate, china, and books." Ignoring the Dashwood ladies' financial and emotional losses, "she could not help feeling it hard that as Mrs. Dashwood's income would be so trifling in comparison with their own, she should have any handsome articles of furniture." She watched "the packages depart with a sigh."

---

2. OK, I admit I love the double entendre the name Fanny Dashwood offers. See the last footnote.

As someone who worked retail through college, I have intimate knowledge of how awful women can be to each other when the stakes are low. I've witnessed territorial gift-shop wars when a flock of part-timers fought for sovereignty over a particular product line. I've seen female supervisors only scheduling "the gals" on deep-clean days, ensuring that only women had to swing a mop. In grad school, I watched tenured female professors refuse to communicate with one another for decades over a theory they "owned." Don't get me started on office supply gatekeepers, admin women treating each Post-it or pen as her own.

SOMETIMES IT'S JUST ABOUT WINNING, NO MATTER HOW SMALL THE PRIZE

Maybe that's why the joy I find in *Sense and Sensibility* isn't just because Elinor finally hooks Edward Ferrars. Austen doesn't make him very appealing, being at best called "not handsome." His natural shyness and lack of ambition make him a dud, as heroes go. Undoubtedly, his youthful proposal to Lucy resulted from raging teenage hormones and much coercion. Overall, he's inoffensive, except for leading Elinor on.

The real action of the novel takes place between its women. A chance meeting in London between the two Dashwood factions reveals that the family dynamic is unchanged even after the move to Devon. Still convinced that Elinor is out to snare her brother, Fanny defies social niceties. Instead of immediately paying the Dashwoods a call, she sends her husband to scope out their relations. Only after John confirms that Lady Middleton is wealthy does Fanny condescend to visit. Ever snobbish, Fanny ignores "good-humored, merry, fat" Mrs. Jennings, finding comradery in her titled daughter instead. Austen's narrator shares that "There was a kind of cold-hearted selfishness on both sides, which mutually attracted them; and they sympathized with each other in an insipid propriety of demeanor and a general want of understanding."

Fanny's tactic of not acknowledging her sisters-in-law and excluding them from social conventions like courtesy meetings is a well-documented twenty-first-century workplace bullying tactic. Once again, Fanny is only motivated by money and appearances, beginning a chain of events leading to her inevitable, delicious disappointment.

By this point in the novel, Austen has brought us to the brink. Things cannot possibly get any worse for our beloved Dashwood girls. We've stood by their sides when they retreat to a pokey cottage next to a busybody relative. We have endured the constant attention of Sir Middleton and Mrs. Jennings, and we understand that their only opportunity to travel is to trail those meddlers to the capital. Lucy Steele, that scheming parasite, has killed our dreams for Elinor. Marianne is off in a corner, weeping far too loudly, heartbroken by mercenary Willoughby. Foolish, good-hearted Edward is wearing jewelry made from another girl's hair.

Finally, Lucy's horrible secret becomes something extraordinary.

Knowing something Fanny doesn't opens a valve in us, releasing built-up steam. Finally, we are relieved of some of the awful pressure that caring for fictional characters can bring. Waiting for Fanny's eventual disappointment, my dark little heart warms at her miscalculations.

In *Comeuppance: Costly Signaling, Altruistic Punishment, and Other Biological Components of Fiction*, Professor William Fleisch proposes that this type of information in novels is pleasurable in the same way revenge is. It gives us the upper hand. For Fleisch, it's why we read literature in the first place. It may not be fact, Fleisch maintains, but fiction is very human. It depicts behaviors that every individual can understand according to their own experience, teaching us how to cope in our real lives.

STAY OUT OF OTHER PEOPLE'S LOVE LIVES

Two hundred years after being written, the essence of the Ferrars ladies lingers in the world. Their familiarity is why we delight at their downfall. They are the meddlers, the ones who insert themselves into the romantic relationships of their relatives, thinking they have any business there.[3]

Their smarty-pants attitude makes it pleasurable to know a secret with the potential to shatter their illusions of control. Being in on Lucy's clandestine engagement takes the sting out of watching Fanny and her mother lavish foolish praise on their unknown adversary. Suddenly, the awfulness of their relationship means that Mrs. Ferrars is no longer a threat to our Elinor. She is rendered comical in refusing to speak to our heroine, "whom she eyed with the spirited determination of disliking her at all events."

Suddenly, we can chuckle when Fanny evades speaking of Edward in Elinor's presence, assuming that they were "still so very much attached to each other." Her attempts to divide them in both "word and deed on every occasion" is hysterical. We can gloat when Fanny thinks that nothing would have induced her to say her brother's name in front of Elinor unless to announce his marriage to a suitable heiress.

The joke's on her. We know that Edward's wife-to-be is a penniless, uneducated snake.

Fanny is so oblivious that she invites Lucy and her sister into her home, a privilege withheld from Elinor. Feeling infinitely superior to the Dashwood ladies, Fanny describes the Steeles as "well-behaved, good kind of girls" who deserve her attention. Mrs. John Dashwood considers these uneducated bumpkins safe; Elinor represents danger.

Watching Lucy enter Fanny's household is hugely satisfying. If Fanny knew what we know, she would have met the Steeles with pitchforks and torches. Instead, Fanny rejoices in their arrival, as it makes a visit from Elinor and Marianne impossible. "In her escape" from such a dire circumstance, readers learn that she is "proud of the ready wit that procured it."

---

3. Unless there is violence or abuse involved. Then get in there and meddle. Help. Do whatever you can to get that person to safety and keep them safe.

Clever, indeed.

Our secret mirth continues as Mrs. Ferrars lavishes the Miss Steeles with attention and praise. Elinor herself couldn't help smiling at "the graciousness of both mother and daughter towards the very person—for Lucy was particularly distinguished—whom of all others, had they known as much as she did, they would have been most anxious to mortify."

Of course, Lucy gobbles up the flattery, leading Elinor to question her intelligence yet again. Lucy is obviously only favored because she isn't Elinor. Luckily, our sensible heroine has come to terms with the situation and "could not now be made unhappy by this behavior." Had the scene taken place "a few months ago, it would have hurt her exceedingly; but it was not in Mrs. Ferrars' power to distress her by it now." Instead of being injured by the treatment, it "only amused her."

TRY TO FIND HUMOR WHENEVER YOU CAN

Watching their "graciousness so misapplied" and the "studied attentions with which the Miss Steeles courted its continuance," Elinor has much to teach us. Instead of wallowing in self-pity, she reflects on the "mean-spirited folly from which it sprung." Their egregious behavior has an unintended effect; finally, Elinor can let go of connections between her half-brother's family and her own. Any bonds that may have existed between the separate Dashwood families through their shared father were broken.

Initially, Elinor had hoped to "avoid a breach with their brother" by lingering in Norland after Fanny's arrival. Her "coolness of judgment" and early maturity enabled her to remain in a place no longer her own. Fanny is the nudge Elinor needs to create a new home far away from Norland, along with her mother and two sisters. Lucy's secret pushes Elinor into "thoroughly despising them all four."

Since "a farther connection between the families" could bring nothing but grief, she is finally able to walk away.

Like female relational aggression, sibling estrangement like that of John Dashwood and his stepsisters has only recently attracted scientific attention. Estimates of its ubiquity vary from one-tenth to one-quarter of all US families experiencing a communication standstill between relatives. The reasons vary widely, from politics, issues with the family business, caring for aging parents, unhealed childhood wounds, and contentious wills. It's no wonder that the Dashwood family ties unraveled after the death of their father; they had never been strong.

Sometimes separation is best.

Sometimes it's the only healthy option.

HAPPY ENDINGS ARE WHAT YOU MAKE OF THEM

The hallmarks of Austen's realism continue to the novel's less-than-ecstatically happy end. Elinor and Edward marry quietly, under modest circumstances unheard of in Hollywood. All that Austen allows us is the brief phrase, "the ceremony took place in Barton church early in the autumn."

Austen's fictional families are simultaneously united and divided. We'll never know what personal experience Austen drew on when praising the Dashwood sisters for getting along *despite* "constant communication which strong family affection would naturally dictate." Even Marianne demonstrates level-headed sensibility, as "though sisters, and living within sight of each other," she and Elinor were able to "live without disagreement between themselves" or "producing coolness between their husbands." Happily, even foolish "Mrs. Dashwood was prudent" enough not to move in with either set of newlyweds.

Things don't finish quite as smoothly for the Ferrars family. Grumpy Mrs. Ferrars is presented with two unwanted daughters-in-law, and Fanny certainly doesn't get what she wants. No, as much as I hate Lucy Steele, her happy end doesn't really interest me. Instead, it's rotten Fanny Dashwood's *unhappy* one that makes me smile. In the end, Fanny is the only character significantly punished for her ambitions, and I really, *really* want to put her into a box and leave her there.

She's evil. End of story.

So why do I have niggling doubts?

What do we even know about her? She's a one-dimensional, rapacious mama bear, manipulating her husband into cutting off his stepsisters. To warmhearted Mrs. Jennings, Fanny "appeared nothing more than a little proud-looking woman of uncordial address, who met her husband's sisters without any affection, and almost without having anything to say to them." She spends her time and energy trying to please her mother, who seems even worse. "Upright, even to formality, in her figure, and serious, even to sourness, in her aspect," Mrs. Ferrars eyed Elinor "with the spirited determination of disliking her at all events."

Despite these formidable barricades, Lucy need only invest a little "perseverance in humility of conduct and messages," and "gratitude for the unkindness she was treated with" to achieve "by rapid degrees . . . the highest state of affection and influence" with Mrs. Ferrars. Forgetting all her snobby principles, the matriarch eventually provides "very liberal assistance" to (already) wealthy Robert and his uneducated wife. Selfish twit Lucy becomes "a favorite child" through flattery, and relations between her and Fanny Dashwood are frequently marked by "jealousies and ill-will."

Stop.

How is this possible? How completely unimportant must a daughter be to be usurped so easily by a Lucy Steele? How little real affection does Mrs. Ferrars have for Fanny to be sweet-talked by an obviously ignorant bumpkin? Could this lack of affection be the basis of her profound materialism?

We will never know.

One glimmer of hope for Fanny is that she remained civil with her Dashwood in-laws. "Though she never spoke of it," Elinor did sense that Fanny never forgot the damage caused by her mercenary behavior. It's unlikely the families will meet again apart from the occasional perfunctory dinner in town.

We can only hope that Fanny eventually redeems herself by forgetting her desire for the family china and focusing on friendliness instead.

CHAPTER 9

Mrs. Norris

Depend upon It, It Is Not You Who Is Wanted

down they forgot as up they grew
—E. E. Cummings

It's safe to say that Austen's third published novel, *Mansfield Park*, is divisive. Some love it. Some hate it. Fanny Price, its sickly, goody-goody heroine, is annoyingly passive. She spends her days silently pining for historically accurate and acceptable incest with her cousin. Her parents live in such squalor that visiting them is seen as a punishment rather than a reward. What could be a plodding coming of age story about a lovesick also-ran becomes a tale of intimate family jealousies and harm.

The name of the evil lurking at Mansfield? Mrs. Norris.

Austen's antagonistic aunt is one of her most awful creatures. Her entire life seems to be one of making do—as in making *others* do.

No husband? Spend so much time at your sister's estate that her husband can't help but set you up with one of his friends.

No kids? Selectively spend time with your rich sister's children, especially when it's most lucrative. Mealtimes. Holidays. Provide them with enough compliments to ensure a standing invitation, especially when there's cake.

No cash for groceries? Organize a little family visit to a nearby estate known for its yummy cheese.

No time? Make Fanny run an errand. After all, she has nothing else to do.

ASK MORE QUESTIONS

Fanny's reception at Mansfield reminds me of my first day on the job that inspired this book. I was excited to begin what I thought was my dream job. On paper, it seemed perfect. Despite being selected by a panel of six, including my new boss, her boss, a diversity representative, a union representative, and two potential peers, my welcome was exceptionally chilly.

I was confused. What had happened in the short space between me being offered the job and starting it?

I was expected. There was plenty of work to do. I had the right qualifications and experience, and I was raring to go. I was thrilled to be firmly back in the workforce, having been underemployed while my son was little, and hiring decisions seemed based on his schedule rather than mine.

Within a few hours of clocking in, I sensed that something was drastically wrong. I felt like a disturbance.

On the surface, I had a lot in common with my new boss. About the same age and both new in town, we'd each made our way to Germany on scholarships. We were both passionate about our work, despite sometimes-overcomplicated German employment norms. Privately, we were both raising bilingual children in a provincial and conservative part of the country. As working mothers, we were both navigating our way through a complex, unfamiliar system of schooling and childcare. We both struggled with local beliefs that a mother's place was in the home.

With so many shared challenges and abilities, why did I rub her the wrong way? Like Fanny Price in *Mansfield Park*, my place felt insecure.

Fanny's shabby reception was due to her aunt, Mrs. Norris. The architect of my miserable beginning was my unaccountably hostile manager. I'd thought she'd be relieved to have someone to share her many responsibilities.

I was wrong.

As a shy ten-year-old, Fanny should have received a warm welcome. Instead, she is shunted from pillar to post, enduring a grueling and frightening trip among strangers. In desperate need of nurture and education, Fanny should have been kindly received by the relatives who removed her from the only home she had ever known.

Admittedly, Fanny's extended family isn't close. Her mother is the youngest of three middle-class sisters. The second eldest, indolent but pretty Maria, marries exceptionally well. She becomes the wife of a baronet, Sir Thomas Bertram, and the mistress of swish Mansfield Park. Six years after Maria's astonishingly good match, the eldest sister is "obliged" to marry a poor friend of her brother-in-law, Mr. Norris. Sir Thomas generously provides the pair with a vicarage close to Mansfield.

The youngest sister, Frances—Fanny's mother—follows her heart and marries a handsome, alcoholic naval officer named Price. The pair end up living in relative squalor on the coast, having a multitude of babies they simply can't afford. The childless Mrs. Norris takes affront at her youngest sister's love match, taking it upon herself to write a "long and angry" letter pointing out the "folly of her conduct" and threatening her with all its "possible ill consequences." Not surprisingly, Frances is injured and angry. Who wants to be lectured by an older sister that their life choices are all wrong? A bitter back and forth ensues, resulting in eleven years of silence between the sisters.

Finally, during her ninth (ouch!) pregnancy, an exhausted Mrs. Price gives in. She simply "could no longer afford to cherish pride or resentment, or to lose one connection that might possibly assist her" and her brood. She approaches Lady Bertram, hat in hand, asking for help. Specifically, Mrs. Price asks for assistance with her eldest child, a son. Surely, Sir Thomas had a job for the boy on his West Indian property? Or could make recommendations for an occupation for him out East?

Her ploy backfires. Instead of fetching the boy, the Bertrams send advice, funds, and baby things.

Mrs. Norris isn't so easily satisfied. She can't resist the opportunity to make Frances truly feel the folly of her wanton union. Not supporting the eldest son means that Mrs. Norris could punish Frances doubly; promoting the boy would benefit his misguided parents financially. Instead, Mrs. Norris pushes the Bertram family to take on the one child most likely to help her mother with her numerous small children, the eldest daughter. And so, Mrs. Norris insists on bringing Fanny to Mansfield.

Profiting from Lady Bertram's lethargic apathy, Mrs. Norris has made herself indispensable at the big house through big talk and small deeds. She demonstrably devotes her time and lip service to her four Bertram nieces and nephews. Exerting as little effort as possible, she takes maximum advantage of the family. As shallow as a paddling pool, Mrs. Norris is "thoroughly benevolent," only "as far as walking, talking, and contriving reached." She loves money and knows quite well "how to save her own as to spend that of her friends." Having "no real affection" for the sister she leeched off, she has no trouble taking credit for acts she had no role in carrying out.

Having wormed her way into the Bertrams' daily life, Mrs. Norris orchestrates Fanny's arrival. It seems a compassionate way to ease the Prices' financial burden on the surface. Sir Thomas and his wife assume that the childless Norris couple is looking forward to finally having a young person in their own home, and they are mistaken.

After reaping kudos for the generous suggestion of welcoming Fanny, we learn that "Mrs. Norris had not the least intention of being at any expense whatever in her maintenance." Fanny will have no refuge at the vicarage. Even more, "it had never occurred to" Mrs. Norris, "but as a thing to be carefully avoided." Shy little Fanny Price, it seems, is simply added to the Bertram household.

When determining how Fanny is to be conveyed from Portsmouth to Mansfield, Mrs. Norris orders the help of others. Fanny is to travel to London by coach, "under the care of any creditable person that may chance to be going. I dare say there is always some reputable tradesman's wife or other going up." From there, Mrs. Norris proposes, "I will send

Nanny to London on purpose, and she may have a bed at her cousin the saddler's." Mrs. Norris saves herself both the trouble and the cost.

I can't help but pity poor, unsuspecting Nanny, her cousin, and the poor "suitable" stranger burdened with watching over an unknown child. Things continue in this manner. Fanny's presence won't make a difference upstairs; only servants will bear the brunt of the additional work she represents. Mrs. Norris declares, "it will be just the same to Miss Lee whether she has three girls to teach, or only two—there can be no difference."

I doubt Miss Lee would agree.

Unlike in previous chapters, it's hard to explain Mrs. Norris's behavior in biological terms. Childless, she has no direct genetic inheritance to protect. "Somewhat delicate and puny," penniless Fanny and the four Bertram children share the same amount of DNA with their aunt. Nevertheless, Mrs. Norris favors her wealthy nieces for the resources they open to her. How else can she enjoy rich meals in a country estate or lovely day trips in carriages? Psychological investment into the Bertram sisters is much more likely to pay off than kindness to a poor relation.

Mrs. Norris makes her allegiances clear at every opportunity. In grandiose gestures of false generosity, Mrs. Norris proudly boasts to Sir Thomas that "whatever I can do, as you well know, I am always ready enough to do for the good of those I love." She assures him that she will always maintain a difference between Fanny and her Bertram cousins. "Though I could never feel for this little girl the hundredth part of the regard I bear your own dear children, nor consider her, in any respect, so much my own," she declares, "I should hate myself if I were capable of neglecting her."

Nevertheless, neglect Fanny is precisely what Mrs. Norris does.

Neither Mrs. Norris nor Fanny really belongs at Mansfield. Both are outsiders, poor relations tolerated for what good they can bring to the estate. Both must earn their right to exist in the Mansfield household; Mrs. Norris by flattery and arrangements, and Fanny through small errands and quiet companionship to passive Lady Bertram. Mrs. Norris does nothing to encourage the girl. Instead, she shows the "least regard for her niece," keeping the girl as small of a presence as possible. Mrs. Norris, not the Bertrams, assigns Fanny to an unheated attic room, where she would be of "little bother."

Aunt Norris lacks empathy for anyone who doesn't serve her objectives. Through Fanny—an even poorer relation than herself—Mrs. Norris moves up in the imaginary household hierarchy. Having young Fanny at Mansfield entitles her to a sense of superiority that she otherwise lacks. Like her idle sister, she now has someone of her own to commandeer. Through Fanny, Mrs. Norris becomes a decision maker, a gatekeeper, a holder of keys. She can grant or deny Fanny's wishes as she pleases while basking in self-admiration for her "generous" deeds.

Beyond providing services, Fanny doesn't interest her aunts. Always at their beck and call, she carries messages, fetches objects, and makes tea. As the lowest of the low, she is treated as a servant, exploited into action regardless of her health. Unlike her Bertram cousins, Fanny cannot rest without calling attention from Mrs. Norris. A brief spell of sitting results in accusations, with Aunt Norris declaring it "a very foolish trick, Fanny, to be idling away all the evening upon a sofa." Mrs. Norris hypocritically admonishes Fanny "to think of other people," declaring it "a shocking trick for a young person to be always lolling upon a sofa." Spoken loudly enough, Mrs. Norris's criticisms of Fanny could likely serve double-duty as passive-aggressive chastisement of lazy Lady Bertram.

Austen makes it clear that Mrs. Norris is a taskmaster. Despite Fanny's delicate health, she piles on the chores, from "stooping among the roses" to running errands. Anxious to maintain appearances, Mrs. Norris adds insult to injury, claiming that she thought the walk "would rather do her good . . . for there is nothing so refreshing as a walk after a fatigue of that kind."

Where Aunt Norris is loud, Fanny is quiet. Unlike her aunt, Fanny caters to Lady Bertram with little fanfare. In the words of Henry Crawford, she attends her "with such ineffable sweetness and patience," despite "her aunt's stupidity." She works in "that stupid woman's service

. . . with such unpretending gentleness, so much as if it were a matter of course that she was not to have a moment at her own command."

In contrast, Mrs. Norris's not-so-subtle aggression almost hides the fact that she is also a hanger-on. She is not a Bertram. Especially after the death of her husband, she's become a poor relative, just like Fanny. Her position at Mansfield is precarious. How many external dependents can the estate manage, both financially and psychologically? As Maria and Julia leave home and Fanny reaches adulthood, will the Bertrams still need her?

Mrs. Norris's (once) distinct role reminds me of the uncertain occupational status of many businesswomen. Despite decades of advancement, it seems that there is often only one place in the boardroom for a woman. For women of color, the statistics are even worse. Those who reach a position of power are what sociologist Mariann Cooper refers to as "onlys"—representative "tokens" destined to remain in the singular. Tokens are symbolically "different." Instead of being selected based on performance or potential, these individuals are chosen specifically for their gender, sexuality, skin color, or physical disability. Once a "token" is in place, many organizations feel no compulsion to add another.

The co-author of the 2018 LeanIn.org and McKinsey and Company *Women in the Workplace* report, Cooper refers to this phenomenon as "one-and-done." Just the perception of limitation can create a self-fulfilling prophecy. Women hoping to become the "only" are known to gauge their chances against other women instead of the entire candidate pool. Many of them report feeling the need to put in twice as much effort as male colleagues to achieve similar roles. Others admit putting up with blatant chauvinism, not reporting sexual harassment, or giving up on their private lives to be taken seriously as the single, representative female.

HELPING OTHERS DOESN'T HARM YOU

Throughout the novel, Mrs. Norris evinces the "least regard for her niece." She does nothing to develop or promote Fanny as another disadvantaged family member. Instead, she slyly prevents Fanny from having advantages, from basic physical needs to inclusion at events.

English literature scholar Kay Souter calls Mrs. Norris "the foundational sibling hater." Her spite growing over the years, she is a bully. Finally achieving a kind of power of her own, she commits "psychological warfare against a child: constant criticism, denial of dignity, denial of pleasure, denial of comforts." For Mrs. Norris, Fanny is not a person; she is a tool enabling Mrs. Norris to feel superior to someone, anyone. If Mrs. Norris lived today, it's not hard to imagine her "forgetting" to invite Fanny to important team meetings or moving her desk to a cubicle next to the toilet.

Feminist scholars Susan Weisser and Jennifer Fleischner explain that token women like Mrs. Norris "learn the ways of the oppressors in dealing with the world, ways of operating within that world which the more privileged do not have to engage in." It's not always intentional or even conscious. Since women's place in society has varied so considerably over time and across cultures, Weisser and Fleischner say that it shouldn't be a surprise that women "press on each other in such a confounding variety of ways." After all, our positions in life have been dependent on our relations to men for millennia.

For Weisser and Fleischner, families can represent the worst competition between women. Instead of being "comforting or empowering," some can be "quite frequently just the opposite," being "the most private sites of warfare, of expressions of dominance and fields of hierarchical values." The researchers warn that families can be most damaging "when they masquerade as benevolent social extensions of natural relations."

At first, Mrs. Norris's idea of taking on Fanny seems generous, but declines drastically as the little girl matures. Her selfishness climaxes when Fanny refuses to participate in her cousins' questionable play. Mrs. Norris chides her "in a whisper at once angry and audible," declaring herself ashamed of Fanny for making "such a difficulty of obliging your cousins in a trifle of this sort." Remarkably, Fanny stays strong. "I am not going to urge her," replies Mrs. Norris sharply, "but I shall think her a very obstinate, ungrateful girl if she does not do what her aunt and cousins wish her." She repeats her ominous threat, reminding Fanny of her supplicant status. Mrs. Norris declares her "very ungrateful indeed, considering who and what she is."

Once again, Austen makes being an obstinate girl immensely desirable.

The much-debated play feeds Aunt Norris's desire to exploit the Bertrams. She welcomes the event, installing herself at Mansfield, saving her housekeeping and groceries. No matter how mercenary her behavior, Mrs. Norris justifies it for a nameless, imagined general good. "As the whole arrangement was to bring very little expense to anybody, and none at all to herself," Mrs. Norris approved. Not out of real conviction, but because "she foresaw in it all the comforts of hurry, bustle, and importance." She stood to profit from the play, coincidentally being in "particular want of green baize" at the same time offering to make theater curtains in that very fabric.

Mrs. Norris swells with hypocritical pride at taking two bits of spare wood away from the set-building carpenter's ten-year-old son. She also finds it brazen that little Dick Jackson *just happened* to deliver them when "the servants' dinner-bell was ringing." "I hate such encroaching people," she complains, "the Jacksons are very encroaching, I have always said so: just the sort of people to get all they can." She intervenes, demanding, "*I'll* take the boards to your father." "I hate such greediness," she scolds the (likely very hungry) boy.

He "ought to be ashamed of himself," she concludes, damning the boy for behavior she herself is known for. On an excursion to Maria's future marital estate, she "wheedles plants, cheese, and eggs out of the servants." After the ball, she manages things so that all "supernumerary jellies" end up at her home. I don't know about you, but I have never had a supernumerary jelly in my life.

In her haste to profit from any and everything, Mrs. Norris forgets that her role depends entirely on her pug-obsessed sister's laziness. When the Bertram children and Fanny grow up, Mrs. Norris's usefulness wanes. Sir Thomas no longer requires an ersatz homemaker to compensate for his wife's lethargy.

She is shocked to realize that her importance is at an end.

It begins slowly. When her brother-in-law reappears from his trip abroad, he enters the house alone (as you'd expect from a healthy adult). This vexes Mrs. Norris, as "it left her nothing to do." His independent entrance means that she lost the privilege of loudly welcoming him and spreading "the happy news throughout the house." Such a simple act leaves Mrs. Norris feeling "defrauded of an office on which she had always depended, whether his arrival or his death were to be the thing unfolded." The ineffectual widow "was now trying to be in a bustle without having anything to bustle about."

PEOPLE GET WARPED ABOUT THE WEIRDEST THINGS

Later, she is shocked to learn that Sir Bertram distinguishes their niece by throwing a ball in her honor. Despite Mrs. Norris's best efforts, Fanny has managed to earn her uncle's affection. The older woman is incensed. "A ball at such a time! His daughters absent and herself not consulted!" Mrs. Norris quickly recovers after identifying a personal benefit. "There was comfort, however, soon at hand. *She* must be the doer of everything . . . *she* should have to do the honors of the evening."

Mrs. Norris is tolerated by the Bertrams as a necessary evil—*if* she's useful.

Provocatively, literature professor Claudia Johnson likens Austen herself with today's token women. Assessing the author's ascent into the Western canon, Johnson finds that critiques of Austen's work have been "qualitatively different from those of her male counterparts." "Because of it," Johnson cautions, Austen "has been admitted into the canon on terms which cast doubt on her qualifications." Instead of being judged on her own (incredibly deserved) merit, her presence in the canon was long "regarded as an act of gallantry." For many years, Austen was considered an anomaly, an exception to the rule that great authors are men.

The same thinking still pervades the corporate world. While the World Bank indicates that more than 50 percent of women over age fifteen in the United States and United Kingdom work, they remain shut out of top positions. Only thirteen of the *Fortune* Global 500 companies were run by women as of August 2020, representing just 2.6 percent.

TOKENISM DOESN'T STOP AT BEING HIRED

Danish gender and political science researchers Vibeke Nielsen and Mikkel Madsen argue that tokenism has "a significantly negative effect on women's management aspirations across all occupational contexts." Their work on the impact of gender diversity on job satisfaction and retention shows that once hired, token women face "isolation, stereotyping, and other difficulties that restrain their integration in the workplace and even more their ascension up the hierarchies." In the current employees' market that we are in, it pays for companies to pay attention to diversity if nothing else than for the bottom line. Turnover is expensive.

Sadly, Nielsen and Madsen's findings are echoed by a 2019 Florida International University study disclosing that once an institution welcomes a woman on the board, additional appointments reflect "diminishing legitimacy gains." In other words, there is a "one and done" sentiment. "Only" males create no such effect.

Mrs. Norris's reaction to Henry Crawford's proposal is telling. Like those older token women who resent their youthful peers' ascent in corporate life without enduring twentieth-century chauvinist crap, Aunt Norris is "bitterly angry." She's "more angry with Fanny for having received such an offer than for refusing it."

The contrast to Mrs. Norris's own courtship is stark. Unlike Fanny, the eldest Miss Ward had no choice. After being left on the shelf for six years, she was "obliged to be attached to the Rev. Mr. Norris." The best we learn of her husband is that he "was not contemptible." The pair made do on a skimpy salary provided through the kindness of Sir Thomas.

Henry Crawford's offer to Fanny is nothing like Mrs. Norris's romantic compromise. He has an estate, a fortune, and has been the object of admiration of both Bertram girls. Aunt Norris "disliked Fanny" and begrudged "such an elevation to one whom she had been always trying to depress."

Sadly, Mrs. Norris's behavior is shared outside of novels. Women are known to denigrate their same-sex peers when opportunities are limited and—ironically—when attempting to appear unbiased. Counterintuitively, women don't automatically support each other.

In *Woman's Inhumanity to Woman*, Phyllis Chesler relates the results of a study on gender-biased rejection rates of proposals for the National Science Foundation that showed that female economists were much more likely to dismiss grant requests from other women. The basis of the decisions was fear. Women have represented such a tiny minority of economic scholars in the past that some established women fear that helping others would jeopardize their own careers.

Before blaming them, it's essential to understand that the few who have made it into the upper echelons of the discipline have been re-minded *every* day of *every* year of their *entire* academic careers that they are the exception, not the rule. Likewise, literature professor Tara Ghoshal Wallace finds Mansfield Park "essentially, permanently hos-tile." As "a site of competition and exploitation," the estate is the site of "struggles for power and vengeance that match the intensity of social and economic class struggles."

For Mrs. Norris, Fanny will never really deserve the right to a priv-ileged position at Mansfield Park. For years she alone enjoyed a niche position there. Fanny's development into adulthood—and establish-ment as a loved niece—eventually forces her into reaffirming her rights at every turn.

Refreshingly, Mrs. Norris is one of Austen's few mean characters who get a comeuppance. By contriving the match between libidinous Maria and foolish Mr. Rushford, Mrs. Norris had hoped to ingratiate herself into a new, wealthy household. Instead, it's her downfall.

Maria runs off with Henry Crawford at the first opportunity. As a damaged woman in Regency England, Maria was to have "no second spring of hope or character." She was to disappear, taking the egregious Mrs. Norris with her.

Instead of being angry with her Bertram niece, Mrs. Norris blames Fanny for not keeping Henry Crawford happy. Who cares if he would have cheated on her with her cousin at every family reunion?

In the end, she is packed off with her slut-shamed niece, "an altered creature, quieted, stupefied, indifferent to everything that passed," reduced so low as to be "benumbed." The pair spend the rest of their lives in "another country, remote and private." "Shut up together with little society, on one side no affection, on the other no judgment," and clearly no more hope of supernumerary jellies, "it may be reasonably supposed that their tempers became their mutual punishment."

Finally, Mrs. Norris is "unable to direct or dictate, or even fancy herself useful." Her reward for meddling? "She was regretted by no one at Mansfield . . . not even Fanny had tears for Aunt Norris, not even when she was gone forever."

The lesson I take from Mrs. Norris is probably one of the most important Austen offers:

IT'S NOT ABOUT YOU

People mostly think about themselves. Of course, it's hard not to take things personally, but the reality is that each one of us is the center of our very own universe. Trying to force Fanny to marry Henry Crawford has nothing to do with Fanny or Henry.

It's about power.

The ability of women like Mrs. Norris to disassociate from other women can "constrain and undermine women's progress," according to business management experts Sharon Mavin, Gina Grandy, and Janine Williams. In their work on elite women leaders, they find relationships between working women "complex, contradictory, and under-researched." Applying what they refer to as "intra-gender micro-violence," women like Mrs. Norris have no problem suppressing others' opportunities to advance their own. The problem is inherently gendered, they contend.

Writing this book and reading Jane Austen, I now realize that my boss's behavior had nothing to do with me. Just like the damage Aunt Norris inflicted, her actions were about her. It can't have been fun being the eldest, having to watch her passive younger sister marry a rich man. It was probably awful being forced to linger at home with her parents while little-miss-laziness Lady Bertram got to set up a fantastic house and make lovely, spoiled babies. After birthing four strong children, she leads a life of leisure, napping on couches and playing with her pugs.

Like my boss, both Mrs. Norris and Mrs. Price are forced to live frugally. The one advantage the Prices have is having known passion in their youth. Despite (or because of) the tininess of their home, the pair are astonishingly fertile, producing enough children to spare a few in service of Lady Bertram. Poor Mrs. Norris marries out of desperation. She keeps her household together with little means and big tricks. After her husband dies, she is forced to relinquish the rectory for a modest house, defending her right to the luxury of a spare room.

I'm sure that Mrs. Norris convinces herself that this is unfair, and prides herself at making do at the expense of others. Saving money and denying pleasure for the thrill of efficiency become her life's work. It's no wonder nobody misses her when she is gone.

My boss's reward for her off-putting behavior? A constant turnover of staff.

In retrospect, I doubt I could have done anything to win her favor. Like Fanny and Mrs. Norris, both poor relatives, my boss and I were a little too alike for comfort. We each brought similar strengths and work experience. The critical difference between us was highly personal; while my son was already in school, her daughter was in the dark days of inadequate childcare provisions for single mothers. Her struggle was ever present, from having to bring her sick child to work to slipping out of meetings that ran over schedule to pick her up on time. Like Mrs. Norris, she often seemed "solitary, helpless, and forlorn," not even trying to put on a brave face about her quite understandable frustrations. She did not accept my help.

Having a partner meant that I could do things that her strict schedule prohibited. My flexibility meant that although I was her subordinate, I could represent the department at evening functions and off-site events. I could work until my desk was clear. My son could recover from a cold at home, in his own bed instead of the office couch. My life must have looked cushy from her perspective.

Like Fanny to her aunt, I felt "charged as the demon of the piece."

Most of you realize that "cushy" isn't a word often associated with raising small children. Like many working moms, I felt guilty for not being in two places at once. I simply had the good fortune to hide my inner conflict because I wasn't parenting alone. The pandemic has magnified these feelings for many working moms. Without reliable childcare or trusted support, COVID-19 has resulted in sinking workforce participation rates for women across the globe. When schools and daycare facilities close, women pick up most of the slack. Even after vaccines became available, many simply couldn't afford to return to work considering the cost of quality childcare. Those who remained at work are reporting unprecedented levels of burnout, according to a 2021 McKinsey study.

In retrospect, my life probably seemed carefree to my emotionally and physically overextended boss. She simply could not afford to allocate her limited resources to welcoming a new employee. My desk was graffitied with coffee rings when I arrived, and my onboarding was nil. I was left to piece together the department's objectives and processes by myself, using past emails and files. She frequently "forgot" to include me on invitations to inter-departmental meetings. Important information wasn't forwarded. Expenses took months to be approved, and deadlines were always last-minute by the time they reached my workstation.

In the end, I left within a year. I had enough career experience to understand her situation and forgive much, but I couldn't bear her frosty volatility. My eventual replacement didn't even make it a month, and it wasn't surprising to learn that the entire department has been emptied since.

Even my bitchy boss is long gone.

Like Maria and Aunt Norris, it was like we were never there.

CHAPTER 10

Lady Catherine de Bourgh

I Take No Leave of You

There is a special place in hell for women
who don't help other women.
—MADELEINE ALBRIGHT

Never in a million years would I have thought that I'd feel sorry for Lady Catherine de Bourgh. It came on so gradually that I hardly know when it began, but I believe I must date it from turning the ripe old age of fifty. Before then, I thought I recognized Lady Catherine for what she was: an over-privileged, over-grown mean girl, throwing her weight around at every opportunity.

The aunt of Mr. Darcy, the hunky hero of *Pride and Prejudice*, Lady Catherine is a minor character with significant impact. She's the worst: Austen's very own Cruella De Vil, White Witch, Bellatrix Lestrange. For the longest time, I viewed her as Austen's own proto-Karen. The resemblance is striking. Both share the same self-seeking habit of lashing out at anyone they see as impinging on their perceived rights. Of course, Lady Catherine would call the manager if she didn't feel that service was up to snuff. I've no doubt that she would have decimated local toilet paper supplies for her personal backside at the merest hint of a pandemic-related shortage. Re-reading Austen's most popular novel the umpteenth time, compassion was the last thing on my mind.

Then, I became invisible.

AGE AFFECTS EYESIGHT (AND INSIGHT)

At first, with the onset of middle age, female invisibility felt miraculous, like a secret superpower. After decades of creepy male stares, inappropriate comments, and unwanted advances, it was a relief to be rid of them. I'll never stop carrying my car keys like makeshift weapons at night, but invisibility can be liberating. Strange men don't consider me a fuckable woman, and that's fine with me.

What isn't so fun is that some women fail to see me as well.

It's not *all* bad. The first time I consciously remember feeling uncomfortable about my body was after a relative's comments. She loved to point out "Sarah's new little boobies" at the pool, remarks only slightly less cringeworthy than her monthly announcement that "Sarah got her little friend." Dying inside, I had no idea how to react. Being able to disappear back then would have felt like a miracle.

Thirty-some years later, when a new intern wouldn't look me in the eye, I wasn't grateful. Going around the conference room table introducing ourselves, she visibly tuned out at my turn. For her, I simply didn't exist.

Was it my accent?

My matronly figure?

I stealthily sniffed under my arm. I was pretty sure I didn't smell bad.

Before you call me paranoid, I should mention that noticing behavior has been part of my job for over twenty years. After my master's degree in art history at a state university, I fell into a career in Human Resources (as one does). Since then, I've spent countless hours analyzing people's body language, eye contact, and interpersonal skills as part of recruiting. Where people sit and how they speak can be very telling during job interviews and assessment centers, and it's a habit that has spilled over into my private life. It's not a trait that makes me popular, but I enjoy it just the same.

For one solid year, I watched the lovely young intern *not* see me. She wasn't unfriendly. She just had absolutely no interest in me. She'd go to anyone *but* me for feedback or direction. Truth be told, the situation bothered me much more than I'd like to admit.

The same thing began happening in shops and restaurants around the same time. Until then, I'd always put it down to the German lack of customer service and general discomfort with small talk. Being ignored by that intern made me face facts. I would never again be the cute young international colleague or star student. I wouldn't even be just a (smooth and unwrinkled) pretty face.

Suddenly, I had a better understanding of Lady Catherine de Bourgh.

I strongly suspect that Austen's bitchy matriarch felt the same way I did when a chit of a girl turned up in her enviable home, refusing to play by her (or society's) rules. Well past the bloom of youth, Lady Catherine surrounded herself with people who kowtowed to her status and wealth. Until Elizabeth Bennet arrived, she had never questioned her visibility, patronage, and presence.

Her title offers clues about her youth. In Mr. Collins's first letter to Mr. Bennet, he boasts that Lady Catherine is the daughter of a peer. His use of "honorable," "Lady," and her first name along with that of her husband's family indicates that Lady Catherine married beneath her—at least in social status terms. Although clearly extremely rich, Sir Lewis de Bourgh was no peer of the realm. Instead, his mere "Sir" indicates that either he or a male ancestor bought the title of baronet.

Following King James the First, monarchs used the baronetage to raise funds. Through the charmingly nicknamed "cash for coronets" system, wealthy men could gain a title to pass on to their eldest legitimate male heir in exchange for financing a group of soldiers or settlers. Just how Sir Lewis obtained his title invites speculation. There certainly wasn't a lack of battles with Bonapartes to be fought at that time. Alternatively, British explorers were opening new places to colonize and rob of their rich natural resources. Settlers were needed to ensure the British occupation of outposts on far-flung continents. With so many wars and enticing opportunities for exploitation, it's no wonder the seventeenth and eighteenth centuries witnessed a surge of baronets.

Lady Catherine's sister Anne married even lower in terms of social hierarchy. While exorbitantly land-rich for several generations, the Darcy family is common. Mr. Darcy's mother retained the right to be called "Lady" but not to pass the title down to her children.

It's fun to imagine teenage Catherine and Anne, late-eighteenth-century "it girls," driving around town in the coolest carriages. As two titled, privileged daughters of a peer of the realm, they were probably pursued by a slew of bachelors, drawn to their pedigrees and purses. It's doubtful that their looks or personalities mattered. An alliance with one of them guaranteed entrance into circles only accessible by noble birth. Fabulous estates like Rosings Park and Pemberley were the price that had to be paid.

Although we don't know Lady Anne Darcy's story, readers have a privileged glimpse into Lady Catherine's unusual autonomy. Regency readers could assume that characters like Lady Catherine were accustomed to having their demands met. For wealthy women like her, a dead husband guaranteed a position in society. As the largest employer in the area, keeping her sweet was the price many had to pay to keep their jobs and homes. Cultural historian Mary Poovey tells us that this rare combination of title and riches ensures Lady Catherine's right to misbehave.

Likewise, she could expect her daughter to be considered a great catch, regardless of her state of health. Historian Lawrence Stone tells us that at the time, it was plausible for her to have a say in her daughter's and orphaned nephew's marriage. Stone explains that influential parents had "the right of veto over socially or economically unsuitable candidates."

No wonder Lady Catherine tells Elizabeth Bennet to push off. After all, she and her equally entitled sister made a pact over little Anne de Bourgh's cradle. The opinions of Fitzwilliam and baby Anne were of no interest. Planning to merge the two vast fortunes, Lady Catherine keeps her daughter at home, malleable and under her control. Lady Catherine could retain authority by unifying the cousins, becoming the de facto mistress of both Rosings Park *and* Pemberley. With that settled, Lady Catherine had no compulsion to advertise her daughter in society.

What she didn't consider was the radical shift taking place on the Regency marriage market. Suddenly, children were making their own choices based on affection rather than the dictates of their families. In *Pride and Prejudice*, Lady Catherine is alone. Her husband and sister have both passed, leaving her in possession of a vast home, reigning over "superlatively stupid" conversations between her sickly daughter and their servant. After a lifetime of being special, she is sidelined. The less she is listened to, the louder she gets.

Like me, Lady Catherine has become invisible.

HIGH SCHOOL IS FOREVER

This tiresome truth turns Lady Catherine into the micromanaging Queen Bee so familiar to Austen fans. Unlike the teenage Queen Bees of Rosalind Wiseman's research explored in previous chapters, Lady Catherine follows the pattern of adult twenty-first-century boardroom bullies. They superglue the shards of glass left in their wake, ensuring that any woman following them faces the same barriers they had. These Queen Bees aren't satisfied at blocking the advancement of junior colleagues but have been shown in numerous studies to be intolerant of competition from their female peers.

Initially, the term "Queen Bee Syndrome" described the tendency of successful women to oppose the women's liberation movement. Although it has since expanded to encompass businesswomen hindering career advances for their peers, its original meaning retains resonance. It comprises women like the ultra-conservative, anti-feminist, and anti–Equal Rights Amendment attorney Phyllis Stewart Schlafly (1924–2016). Schlafly herself enjoyed a political leadership position but endorsed keeping other women in the kitchen and legally subject to their husbands' whims (or violence) in the bedroom.

Dutch psychologist Belle Derks explains that this behavior isn't inevitable. Instead, Derks finds that it's triggered by situations where women's presence is rare and frequently subject to gender discrimination and negative stereotyping. Citing numerous psychological studies from over almost two decades, Derks finds that instead of championing their female peers, these women learn to identify with the male majority surrounding them. A similar phenomenon is seen among other "minorities" in such positions, whether LGBTQ+ or people of color. Think of it as a kind of occupational Stockholm Syndrome.

From the start, Austen describes Lady Catherine in less than feminine terms. At her very first meeting with Elizabeth, she is introduced as "a tall, large woman, with strongly-marked features, which might once have been handsome. Her air was not conciliating, nor was her manner of receiving them such as to make her visitors forget their inferior rank." Thoroughly convinced of herself, "she was not rendered formidable by silence, but whatever she said was spoken in so authoritative a tone, as marked her self-importance."

In oppressively patriarchal Regency Britain, it's no stretch to interpret Lady Catherine as someone unlikely to be sympathetic to other women. So many of her contemporaries were struggling financially that even her great wealth couldn't make a significant difference. Like the women cited in Derks's studies, she was much more likely to identify with the powerful men around her than other women.

Two hundred years later, women remain excluded from the upper echelons of what is seen as a male domain. According to a 2020 UN Development Program survey of data from seventy-five countries representing 80 percent of the global population, *nine out of ten people* hold a bias against women. Not just men, *people*. Not only do we women face prejudice from 91 percent of men, but also 86 percent of women report holding "at least one bias against women in relation to politics, economics, education, violence, or reproductive rights."

These shocking results indicate a lack of gender equality in political and economic power and a lack of personal agency for a *significant* percentage of women worldwide. No wonder women continue to face occupational scarcity. While the *Harvard Business Review* reports more women in managerial roles than ever before, these tend to be in lower-paid, "pink ghetto" categories: social and community service, education administration, real estate, and (ha!) human resources. Women still make up less than 10 percent of architecture, IT, engineering, and construction managers. Lack of education isn't the problem. Instead, hiring managers cite a "lack of fit." Women who do manage entry into underrepresented disciplines face tokenism, glass ceilings, or glass cliffs.

INSECURITY BREEDS MICROMANAGEMENT

In occupational terms, Lady Catherine's insecurity turns her into the cliché of a micromanager, fixated on supervising those around her to the smallest detail. Business professor Richard D. White calls micromanaging a disease. Comparing them to addicts and alcoholics, White explains that they "are the last people to recognize that they are hooked on controlling others." Indeed, Austen tells us that "nothing was beneath" Lady Catherine's attention, "which could furnish her with an occasion of dictating to others." As the mistress of Rosings Park, she feels entitled to examine Charlotte's "domestic concerns familiarly and minutely," giving "a great deal of advice as to the management of them all." Lady Catherine tells Mrs. Collins how "everything ought to be regulated," going so far as to instruct her "as to the care of her cows and her poultry."

Lady Catherine regularly descends on Charlotte's household, scattering unrequested remarks before her. "Nothing escaped her observation that was passing in the room during these visits. She examined into their employments, looked at their work, and advised them to do it differently." She "found fault with the arrangement of the furniture; or detected the housemaid in negligence." Instead of being pleased by Charlotte's hospitality, "if she accepted any refreshment," she "seemed to do it only for the sake of finding out that Mrs. Collins's joints of meat were too large for her family."

Things seem even more dire for the villagers. Although she "was not in commission of the peace of the county," Lady Catherine takes it upon herself to address even "the minutest concerns of which were carried to her by Mr. Collins." Ludicrously, readers learn that "whenever any of the cottagers were disposed to be quarrelsome, discontented, or too poor, she sallied forth into the village to settle their differences, silence their complaints, and scold them into harmony and plenty."

According to White, micromanagers tend to hire drones like Mr. Collins. His bumbling obsequiousness enables Lady Catherine's behavior. Bosses like her resist hiring talented employees who may challenge them. The long-term result, White explains, is a workforce so afraid of constant criticism that it "no longer take(s) risks, creativity dries up, and customer service goes down the drain." Rosings Park is just such an environment. Miss de Bourgh is "pale and sickly," speaking "very little, except in a low voice, to Mrs. Jenkinson, in whose appearance there was nothing remarkable."

Finding such a grateful, obedient servant like Mr. Collins to be the rector of her local parish is a godsend. Every fiber of his being exudes "extraordinary deference for Lady Catherine." Almost every move he makes includes a reference to his mighty patroness. She is the first topic of his letters and conversation at dinners. Unable to resist loud comparisons to the finery found at Rosings Park, Mr. Collins quickly offends all around him at evening card parties and balls. Through him, she is seen, if only for her wealth.

REAL VALUE DOESN'T COME FROM MONEY

Lady Catherine is shocked to find a much different reception in his cousin Elizabeth, who has no interest in her antics. Why should she? Lady Catherine is a bully. She unsuccessfully attempts to convey an almost royal presence when she invites the Meryton party to her home for dinner. "With great condescension," she "arose to receive them." Initially, she's "gratified by their excessive admiration" of her house, yet throughout the evening, she self-importantly speaks "without any intermission," "delivering her opinion on every subject in so decisive a manner, as proved that she was not used to have her judgment controverted."

Lady Catherine freely admits to lacking traditional feminine accomplishments. Mary Poovey explains that skills such as "piano playing, singing, dancing, fine needlework, and painting" were, for the average Regency gentleman's daughter, the only "legitimate vehicle for the indirect indulgence of vanity." In essence, they were "only thinly disguised opportunities for the display of personal charms."

Lady Catherine assumes she's beyond comparison, probably because she never was compared to others. Unlike the less affluent damsels of the day, she never had to learn to play an instrument, net a bag, or cover a screen. Instead, her social and economic status allows her to make broad statements like, "if I had ever learnt, I should have been a great proficient." Despite her lack of knowledge, Lady Catherine doesn't hesitate to instruct others, remarking "on Elizabeth's performance, mixing with them many instructions on execution and taste." Putting Elizabeth in her place, Lady Catherine offers to let her "come to Rosings every day and play on the pianoforte in Mrs. Jenkinson's room." After all, in the servants' quarters, "she would be in nobody's way."

Bless her heart.

This tone continues throughout Elizabeth's visit. Lady Catherine demands her guests admire her possessions at every opportunity. She sends each visitor, one by one, to a separate window to admire the view. When her visitors echo Mr. Collins's overblown compliments, she gratifies them with smiles, performing lengthy monologues at every opportunity. Her unique position affords her the *chutzpah* to pose inappropriately personal questions of Elizabeth.

Apart from Mr. Collins, it suddenly seems that no one paid Lady Catherine much attention. Sensing her invisibility, she simply cannot tolerate conversations from which she is omitted. Repeatedly, she calls out, demanding to know what others are talking about. Unasked, she makes grand proclamations of her knowledge on issues.

Women like Lady Catherine are reminiscent of women studied by Belle Derks and her colleagues. They find that "senior women in masculine organizational cultures" have in the past achieved their positions "by dissociating themselves from their gender." Working with nearly one hundred female Dutch senior managers, they found that Queen Bee Syndrome is an individual response. Low gender-identified women react to gender discrimination by joining the perpetrators; it becomes a vicious cycle.

It seems that abusive behavior among female employees increases as they climb the career ladder. Sociologist Marianne Cooper argues that various attitudes shape Queen Bee Syndrome. First, some women belittle other women for demonstrating habits typically considered "feminine," such as being "too emotional." Other women attempt to appear more masculine, claiming to identify more with the patriarchy through statements such as "I think like a guy," or by claiming to have "only male friends."

Alternatively, some Queen Bees deny the very existence of gender discrimination. They claim that women are "just less committed to their careers" than men, calling the legitimacy of gender diversity initiatives into question. For Cooper, "the ultimate Queen Bee is the successful woman who undermines her women colleagues instead of using her power to help other women advance."

In "Sisters at Arms," an investigation of female competition and aggression in the workplace, management experts Leah Sheppard and Karl Aquino consider female aggression a self-fulfilling prophecy. Instead of examining dime-a-dozen male miscreants, media attention is focused on the rare but remarkable Queen Bee. The scarcity of women on corporate boards magnifies gender transgressions.

Media also plays a huge role in perpetuating the Queen Bee stereotype. Pointing to feminist backlash over CEO Marissa Mayer's 2013 edict ending home offices at Yahoo!, Sheppard and Aquino demonstrate how women who display agency are considered cold. Some earn the description "conniving, unsupportive, and backstabbing." Men flexing similar leadership muscles don't get this kind of flack. Instead, they are just doing their jobs.

Expert in contemporary female aggression, psychologist Tracy Vaillancourt asserts that today's "women are still willing to cut each other's throats over what they value most," including jobs, men, and social approval. Her findings echo a 2017 report from the Workplace Bullying Institute. Of over a thousand American adults surveyed, one-fifth had personally experienced abuse in the workplace. Whether the perpetrator was male or female, the victims were significantly more likely to be women.

In Elizabeth Bennet, Austen gives us a heroine who isn't intimidated by Queen Bee de Bourgh. Maybe it's because she grew up in a home surrounded by other strong-willed women and girls. When asked her age, she's playful and evasive. At this, "Lady Catherine seemed quite astonished at not receiving a direct answer." In fact, "Elizabeth suspected herself to be the first creature who had ever dared to trifle with so much dignified impertinence."

In his psychological analysis of Austen's work, Bernard Paris aptly explains, "one senses that Elizabeth has steeled herself to this situation so as to maintain her sense of equality with Lady Catherine." Paris calls Elizabeth's composure "a form of triumph." Discovering Lady Catherine to be "a fool, she becomes completely at her ease and even toys with her adversary by refusing immediately to disclose her age." Elizabeth is fully aware that Lady Catherine is a prominent person yet recognizes her manipulative nature. As a result, "Elizabeth's satisfaction in trifling with her is evident."

Sadly, many modern professional women find it hard to replicate Lizzy's confidence. Subjection to a micromanager is disheartening, especially if one's livelihood is dependent on keeping the oppressor in power sweet. The work of management researcher Giselle Castillo may explain reader gratification at Elizabeth's complete disinterest in performing for Lady Catherine. Castillo finds that 90 percent of her subjects reported working under a micromanager, resulting in feelings of fear, stress, low morale, and little job satisfaction. A significant proportion admitted of switching departments, roles, or companies to escape perpetrators.

NICE PEOPLE NEVER ASK "DO YOU KNOW WHO I AM?"

It's a vicarious delight when Elizabeth continues not to care when Lady Catherine shows up to Longbourn uninvited. Lizzy is admirably unimpressed by Lady Catherine's domineering outbursts and demands. While the older woman feels entitled by rank to aggress openly against Elizabeth and her mother, they don't engage.

Hoping to hear Elizabeth deny an engagement to her nephew, Lady Catherine ignores a long list of social niceties. First, she shows up "too early in the morning for visitors," entering the room "with an air more than usually ungracious," and making "no other reply to Elizabeth's salutation than a slight inclination of the head." She sits down without saying a word, "making no request of introduction," despite the flustered Mrs. Bennet having "received her with utmost politeness."

Lady Catherine seems to have lost any filter she may have once had, asking only after a long silence for information on the persons before her. Unbidden, she proceeds to criticize the room, calling it "most inconvenient." Bulldozing her way into the household, Lady Catherine declines an offer of refreshment, responding "not very politely" and "more than usually insolent and disagreeable." She then proceeds to open doors throughout the home, making unbidden pronouncements on their suitability and size. Once in the garden, the older woman demands information "in an angry tone," warning Elizabeth that she is "not to be trifled with." Insinuating mistrust in Elizabeth, Lady Catherine boasts that her character has "been celebrated for its sincerity and frankness" and intent to make her sentiments known.

Elizabeth is baffled by the attention, and Lady Catherine does not change that. In the words of psychologist Joyce Benenson, women like her "have little incentive to invest in other women," so most of them benefit from punishing ambitious peers.

Punishing Elizabeth is precisely what Lady Catherine plans to do. Unwilling to recognize Elisabeth as an equal, she declares her a "young woman without family, connections, or fortune." Elizabeth wants none of that, reminding Lady Catherine of her position as a gentleman's daughter. Immediately, the senior woman attempts to reinstate the social distance, questioning, "Who was your mother? Who are your uncles and aunts? Do not imagine me ignorant of their condition," as if they were lepers, not respectable members of society.

There's simply no reason for Lady Catherine to collaborate with lower ranks or non-kin women like the Bennets. Repeatedly, the matriarch emphasizes Elizabeth's "presumption," "inferior birth," and mere existence as having no importance whatsoever. She sees no need for her nephew to attach himself to such a family, relying on her status to get what she wants. Time and again, the matriarch reminds Elizabeth of her position, asking, "Miss Bennet, do you know who I am?" proclaiming that she has "not been accustomed to such language," and feeling "entitled to know" all of Darcy's "dearest concerns."

Citing studies of female European university faculty, board members, and police officers, Derks and her colleagues suggest that Lady Catherine's posturing is typical. Unlike males, senior female managers often exhibit a need to describe themselves in terms of status, competitiveness, and assertiveness. In this way, they distance themselves from less successful women and assimilate into male-dominated organizations.

Ironically, it's Lady Catherine's unwillingness to share the spotlight with other women that makes her invisible. As Belle Derks explains, occupational Queen Bees like her are only willing to recognize other members of "the tiny pool of women in similar situations of power." By refusing to identify with their juniors, they perpetuate the scarcity of such roles, limiting opportunities for exchange and assistance. The de Bourgh bully renders herself obsolete.

She creates her own cage by holding herself above everyone else.

Taking another stab at killing Elizabeth's rebellious spirit, Lady Catherine brings up the damage Lydia's bungled elopement has brought to the entire Bennet family. Challenging Elizabeth, she appeals, "I am no stranger to the particulars of your youngest sister's infamous elopement . . . is such a girl to be my nephew's sister?" During the Regency, reputation was a girl's most significant cultural asset. Lady Catherine has no doubts about what went down between Lydia and Wickham. Alluding to her as "such a girl" is a thinly veiled reference to Lydia's loss of innocence. It's not surprising when Lady Catherine demands, "Are the shades of Pemberley to be thus polluted?" referring to Lydia's slapdash marriage to the steward's son.

To this day, women's sexual reputations impact how other women treat them. In a *New York Times* article, John Tierney proposes that slut-shaming is a big part of the "Cold War fought between women." Citing anthropologist Sarah Blaffer Hrdy's groundbreaking work on female behavior, Tierney explains that since men covet sex, some "women limit access as a way of maintaining an advantage in the negotiation of this resource." As a result, any woman who seems to be offering sexual intercourse too readily compromises "the power-holding position" of the entire group. Tierney claims the behavior is why many women disdain peers who are or seem to be loose with their affections. The same kind of slut-shaming is scarce for promiscuous men. After all, boys will be boys. I'd love to reject Tierney's hypothesis outright, as it feels nonsensical in the modern world. Then I turn on my computer. Or mobile phone. Or television. Or radio. And it is everywhere.

Rosalind Wiseman reiterates this notion, pointing out that although girl power has become a "cultural juggernaut . . . the message that modesty and restraint are the essence of femininity persists." Referring to contemporary feminist research, Wiseman asserts that girls continue to be pressured to be "chaste, quiet, thin, and giving." At the same time, they are encouraged to deny "the desire for sexual pleasure, voice, food, and self-interest."

In contrast, boys in US schools are not policed for their hankerings in the same way. Schoolgirls in the United States continue to be monitored for how they dress based on its impact on their male peers. Administrators claim that it is distracting, worrying about its effect on boys' ability to concentrate. Instead of encouraging guys not to see every flash of pubescent skin as an invitation to sexualize their female peers, school administrators force girls to cover up. Not for their own sake, but because of the poor, easily frenzied teenage male.

Likewise, Lady Catherine lectures Elizabeth instead of her lovesick nephew, securing the marriage she hoped to prevent. Of course, she'll gloss over this in the narrative she tells herself. Like Queen Bee managers requiring younger colleagues to match them in aspirational suffering, Lady Catherine will never believe Elizabeth's right to become Mrs. Darcy. The mistress of Rosings Park may visit Pemberley after their wedding, but only to see for herself how Elizabeth falls short. To the end of her days, Lady Catherine will always maintain that Elizabeth's "arts and allurements" drew her nephew in.

We shouldn't forget Anne de Bourgh. Who knows if she was hot to marry her cousin. It's Austen's treatment of Anne that leads literary Darwinist Joseph Carroll to accuse the author of "a certain streak of brutality." "Sickly and peevish" Miss de Bourgh receives no attention. Only her (paid) governess has time for her. Referring to Darwin, Carroll claims that Austen "sacrifices Miss de Bourgh on the altar of the ruthless principle of fitness." By describing Darcy's cousin in terms of weakness and passivity, Austen delivers a sharp contrast to Elizabeth's robust health (and the confident sex drives of her mother and sisters!). Neither Elizabeth nor her creator expresses any emotions toward the girl except that of "vindictive content."

Poor little rich girl Anne, it seems, has been invisible since birth.

Even her mother doesn't see her.

It is precisely this pervasive invisibility that softened me somewhat to the de Bourgh women. Since vanishing myself, it's easier to understand why Lady Catherine attempts to be part of every conversation around her. Her visibility in the world has ebbed and flowed with each distinctive phase of life, and it seems that wealth, beauty, status, and respect are not constant.

From personal experience, it can be a shock to realize that absolutely no one is interested in how you think or feel. At the very least, Austen shows us that, in the end, anonymity is universal. Even prosperous women like Lady Catherine are forced to bribe weary travelers with the promise of dinner and a peek at her top-quality fireplaces to lure them in.

Right or not, studies of older women like Lady Catherine (and me) show that in the West, any deviation from accepted standards of beauty is interpreted negatively. Slim youthfulness, unblemished health, and (sadly) whiteness continue to be the standards against women are measured throughout their lives. It's no wonder that many modern women feel that appearance and fertility are a considerable part of what is expected of them.

Plucking my newly acquired chin hairs, I know how they feel.

FIND NEW WAYS TO SHINE AND TO SEE THE WOMEN AROUND YOU

Finding new forms of visibility later in life can pose a challenge for many women. By clinging to her old expectations of instant recognition and admiration, Lady Catherine could remain ignored until the end of her days. I'd like to think that my intelligence, charm, and sense of humor will save me from a similar fate, but you never know.

I'd love to relate a positive conclusion to my situation at work, but I can't. That young woman never began seeing me as a valuable resource. Instead of being admired for my long career and varied tapestry of experience, I remained invisible. Despite my attempts to include her in projects and learning opportunities, her focus firmly remained on our male boss and youthful colleagues.

Her (hopefully) unconscious snub did serve a purpose. It inspired in me a phase of self-reflection, leading to a new sense of gratitude for the many opportunities I had at her age. I loathe the idea that my gender, youth, and appearance played a crucial role in them, but being invisible made me reconsider. I've had my day as a young intern. My grades were good, my professors liked me, and I was a reasonably attractive white girl with lots of energy and time on my hands. Right or wrong, hiring me posed no challenges for my many middle-aged white male bosses.

After years of establishing myself in my career, I've also discovered for myself the joy of hiring people early in their work lives. I may be invisible to them but watching them grow as professionals and people can be incredibly rewarding. I'll do my best to remember the invisible specter of Lady Catherine when I work with them, behaving as generously to them as I would expect for the Elizabeth Bennets of the world. Moving forward, it's also my responsibility to make sure that those opportunities are available to *everyone*, not just those who remind me of my younger self.

As a parent, I've also learned that young people's self-assured disregard for "old people" isn't personal. It's simply part of their development. Remember what I said about the prefrontal cortex? Any time a teenager tries to instruct you on the "realities" of the world, try to remember it and be forgiving.

YOU MAY BE INVISIBLE TO OTHERS— DON'T BECOME INVISIBLE TO YOURSELF

Austen herself was almost a victim of visibility's volatility. From her gravestone in Winchester Cathedral, no one would know that she was a genius of English literature, as the epitaph memorializes her simply as the "youngest daughter of the late Rev George Austen, formerly Rector of Steventon in this County." Apart from a single reference to the "endowments of her mind," her final resting place is that of an ordinary, albeit devout Christian woman, known for her "charity, devotion, faith and purity."

Austen's ultimate lesson in Lady Catherine, as well as her novels? Visibility in this world is a fluid experience, especially for women. Instead of clutching to past luster, it's crucial to find new ways to shine beyond outward appearances or economic power. Then, as now, our most important visibility is found in ourselves—being able to look ourselves in the mirror every morning, proud of what we put in the world.

A pearl of bonus wisdom? Don't forget to *see* the women around you. Everyone is struggling somehow. A kind word and an open heart can work wonders.

Part IV

HAPPY ENDINGS?

CHAPTER 11

Anne Elliot

Her Happiness Was from Within

You could not shock her more than she shocks me;
Beside her Joyce seems innocent as grass.
It makes me most uncomfortable to see
An English spinster of the middle-class
Describe the amorous effects of "brass,"
Reveal so frankly and with such sobriety
The economic basis of society.

—W. H. Auden

At last, we come to Anne Elliot, one of Austen's most fiercely beloved characters. Initially, I hadn't planned on including the heroine of *Persuasion* in this book. Austen's last completed novel doesn't feature any significantly mean girls; rather, a bunch of individuals behaving very believably and very badly.

It was the Janeites who convinced me to take a closer look at the twenty-seven-year-old spinster forced to leave her family home because of Sir Walter Elliot's spendthrift ways. They belong to the privileged class, and banishment from their family seat, Kellynch Hall, simply means removal to lovely rental accommodation in the ancient spa town of Bath.

Despite not including Anne in my initial investigation of relational aggression, participants in my research survey clamored to voice their opinions on her. Quite a few expressed shock that I could leave Anne out of any inquiry into Austen's characters.

"Why not Anne Elliot???" one woman demanded through the ether, concerned that I had simply forgotten her. Others made similar comments, indicating, "for the record, Anne Elliot has long been my favorite Austen heroine," making sure I noted their devotion even though I hadn't asked.

I understand their resentment. There's just something about Anne.

Like Elinor, Elizabeth, and Catherine, she's a *good* person. Unlike them, she is older and a bit wiser. I don't mean the goody-goodness of Fanny Price; simply a level-headed, generous sort of integrity that doesn't crave the spotlight, who selflessly offers to care for a sister's sick child, or springs into action for a foolish girl who inexplicably jumps off a staircase at the Cobb.

For many readers, Anne Elliot seems above relational pettiness, successfully overlooking the insults and injuries she faces every day from those closest to her. She's not your typical heroine. She isn't the picture of beauty. In fact, her looks have faded somewhat over the years, and she is considered by those around her as well past her sell-by date. Like most of us, she's made huge mistakes in life, trusting other people's opinions rather than listening to her own heart.

Nevertheless, we adore her.

If the vehement backlash to the 2022 Netflix adaptation of *Persuasion* has taught me anything, it's not to mess with Anne Elliot. Janeite social media is full of heated debate surrounding the film. "Ruined," "an affront," "a chaotic disaster," and "cringey" are the gentlest descriptors. Many Janeites are "angry" at the "heinous" depiction of their beloved Anne as "a drunk," "a disaster." A frequent meme reads, "all agony, no hope."

Why do we care so much?

ANNE ELLIOT GETS IT RIGHT

Anne is both fallible and relatable. *Anne is one of us.*

In the end, Anne and Austen taught me far more about my own behavior than anyone else's. Like my survey participants, I've learned to cherish the quiet strength of the Anne Elliots of the world. She's the forgotten middle child of pompous Sir Walter Elliot, exemplifying the value of looking beyond appearances. Like many of us bookworms, Anne isn't a popular extrovert. Her own family doesn't have much use for her. Her father considers her "of very inferior value," a "nobody." "Her word had no weight, her convenience was always to give way—she was only Anne."

Her eldest sister pays her no mind, preferring the companionship of a neighbor, the lowly Mrs. Clay. When the family is forced to leave their home, Elizabeth wants Mrs. Clay to accompany her, not Anne. "Nobody will want her in Bath," Elizabeth declares, shunting Anne off for a period of servitude to their hypochondriacal youngest sister, Mary.

Like Elizabeth and Sir Walter, Mrs. Mary Musgrove is only interested in herself. She was "often a little unwell, and always thinking a great deal of her own complaints." She tends to claim Anne "when anything was the matter." Still, Anne isn't resentful. Instead, she's "glad to be thought of some use," as "being claimed as a good" was "at least better than being rejected as no good at all." After all, "Mary was not so repulsive and unsisterly as Elizabeth."

Low praise indeed.

The only person who truly cares for our heroine is her godmother, Lady Russell, who has altered her own life to minister to Anne over the years. "A sensible, deserving woman," Lady Russell settles near Kellynch Hall simply to be near her friend, Anne's mother. Likely noticing that Sir Elliot was a useless peacock, Lady Russell could be relied upon to help raise their three girls. After Lady Elliot's death, she remains in the area. Fortunately, she was well provided for and did not need to marry Sir Walter, "whatever might have been anticipated on that head by their acquaintance."

At the beginning of *Persuasion*, Lady Russell has safeguarded Anne for over a decade, treasuring her as "a most dear and highly valued god-daughter, favorite, and friend." Although she loved all three Elliot girls, "it was only in Anne that she could fancy the mother to revive again."

CHAPTER 11

RECONSIDER GRUDGES

Reading *Persuasion* in my teens and twenties, I felt bitter toward the "steady age and character" of Lady Russell. Ignoring all the good she had done, I resented her for giving Anne lousy advice at a critical point in her life. Early in the narrative we learn that love-starved Anne fell in love with Frederick Wentworth, a young naval officer. She was nineteen, young for a modern marriage but fair game for a Regency union. Nevertheless, Lady Russell persuades Anne to break off their engagement, claiming it was "a wrong thing: indiscreet, improper, hardly capable of success, and not deserving it." Her argument seemed frivolous; Wentworth simply wasn't wealthy enough for Lady Russell. While Anne could ignore her father's indifference, she couldn't disregard the advice of her ersatz mother.

I've read *Persuasion* so often that I can no longer remember when I stopped resenting Lady Russell. It was easy to dismiss her as a snob, the destroyer of Anne's young, romantic dreams. How dare anyone stand in the way of two people "deeply in love"? For me, Lady Russell was the Austen equivalent of a wicked stepmother questioning a mirror— childhood fairy tales taught me that she should instantly be reviled.

What follows the breakup is a long period of making do. Instead of being led off into the forest or fed a poisoned apple, Anne simply languishes, becoming a pawn in other people's lives. Uninteresting for Sir Walter and Elizabeth, Mary Musgrove and her in-laws use Anne as a sounding board for their many complaints. Mary resents her husband's family for failing to recognize her rank in life. The Musgroves find Mary's constant whining tiresome and ridiculous. None show any real interest in Anne, who "played a great deal better than either of the Miss Musgroves," but had "no fond parents to sit by and fancy themselves delighted" by her evening performances. We learn that "excepting one short period of her life, she had never . . . since the loss of her dear mother, known the happiness of being listened to."

Their disinterest doesn't bother Anne as it does Mary. Where her sister was in a huff at the Musgroves' failure to call on Anne immediately,

Anne takes it in stride. Mary is full of what others *ought* to do to mark her status; "Anne had always thought such a style of intercourse highly imprudent." After all, "the two families were so continually meeting, so much in the habit of running in and out of each other's house at all hours," what would it have served?

Slowly, slowly, despite her family, Anne begins to reemerge from her long romantic hibernation after Frederick Wentworth returns to the area. Rich from successful naval battles, Captain Wentworth visits his sister who is renting Kellynch Lodge. Through him, we learn that he is still angry at being rejected, that Anne has grown older, and that she has refused at least one other suitor. Austen shows us how he watches her when no one else does—he alone notices her distress at being climbed on by her nephews, recognizes her fatigue after a long walk, and advocates for her as the most capable to care for an injured-yet-pretty idiot.

FORGIVE

Poor Anne. The incident at the Cobb seems to have sealed Captain Wentworth's destiny as Louisa Musgrove's suitor. What pain it must have caused her to speak of him to Lady Russell when outlining the incident at Lyme. Uncomfortably, Austen tells us that Anne "could not speak the name and look straight forward to Lady Russell's eye" until she had hinted at his attachment to Louisa.

It's at this point that my heart relents a bit toward Lady Russell. "Her heart reveled in angry pleasure, in pleased contempt, that the man who at twenty-three had seemed to understand somewhat of the value of an Anne Elliot, should, eight years afterwards, be charmed by a Louisa Musgrove." Finally, like our generous Anne, I realize that Lady Russell was simply doing her best. Anne Elliot represents the power of letting go and the peace that comes with it.

By now, I'm sure you've realized that this book began out of frustration. Relational aggression from other women has always confused me, and I am by no means alone. Every single peer I have spoken to about my work has encountered something similar. One was brave enough to tell me that I had injured her.

Initially, my curiosity was motivated by anger, wanting to expose those women, to get back at them somehow through oblique references that allowed me to spend considerable amounts of time re-reading Austen novels and watching Colin Firth towel off.

Then Anne shows up, reminding me that a good memory isn't always a good thing. She could have spent decades resenting Lady Russell for poor guidance, but what would that have served? Lady Russell is a good woman, "and if her second object was to be sensible and well-judging, her first was to see Anne happy."

FORGET

Numerous psychological studies show that forgiveness like Anne's (and hopefully my own) can have mental and physical benefits, from reduced stress and anxiety, anger, and depression. Harboring grudges can bring real pain, from raising blood pressure, disturbing sleep, tightening muscles, and triggering autoimmune conditions to name but a few. Be careful rehashing old wounds; you might just exacerbate them.

Of course, the star-crossed lovers reunite at the end (that letter!). As a trusted mentor, Lady Russell was "the only one among them, whose opposition of feeling could excite any serious anxiety." Lady Russell, the architect of Anne's seven years of bad luck, "must" and *did* "learn to feel that she had been mistaken," and "that she had been unfairly influenced by appearances" so long ago. Austen tells us that "there was nothing less for Lady Russell to do, than to admit that she had been pretty completely wrong, and to take up a new set of opinions and of hopes." Why? Because "she loved Anne better than she loved her own abilities."

BLOOD *AND* WATER ARE IMPORTANT

In *Persuasion*, Austen shows us the value of maintaining friendships in lieu of chasing indifferent relations. While her father and sister are out sucking up to their titled cousins, Anne pays a call on her former governess. There, she learns that Mrs. Smith, a beloved schoolmate, was in town. Mrs. Smith was a few years older than Anne and had showed the girl kindness when she was dumped off at boarding school after losing her mother, "whom she had dearly loved." Austen recognizes Anne's pubescent volatility, "suffering as a girl of fourteen, of strong sensibility and not high spirits, must suffer at such a time." Magnanimous Mrs. Smith took the bereaved girl under her wing.

Although the two hadn't seen each other for years, Anne has not forgotten the woman's sympathy and support. Time has not served Mrs. Smith well. Her husband's death brought both financial and physical ruin; nevertheless, she remains cheerful. Anne wonders at her resilience; "here was that elasticity of mind, that disposition to be comforted, that power of turning readily from evil to good." Despite everything, Mrs. Smith had the ability "of finding employment which carried her out of herself."

While Sir Walter and Elizabeth are fawning over an indifferent Lady Dalrymple, Anne bears witness to connections stronger than kinship. Mrs. Smith surrounds herself with generous women. Though poor, she cherishes their strengths, recognizing that her "landlady had a character to preserve, and would not use her ill," and her sister as a gifted nurse and confidante. "Besides nursing me most admirably," Mrs. Smith reports, she "has really proved an invaluable acquaintance," teaching her various handicrafts to supplement her income as well as afford a few charities of her own. She offers sharp contrast to Elizabeth Elliot, whose only notion of reducing expenses means cutting off charity and stiffing local tradespeople.

Austen's message rings loud and clear. True greatness has little to do with birth, wealth, or appearances. Instead, it is what you do for others.

Perhaps Austen is describing herself in the form of Nurse Rooke, who is "a shrewd, intelligent, sensible woman," with a "line for seeing human nature." Mrs. Smith tells us that she is "infinitely superior to thousands of those who having only received 'the best education in the world,' know nothing worth attending to."

Anne tells us precisely the kind of friends to whom she aspires. Instead of scrambling to attention at the hint of a Dalrymple drop-in, she appreciates real exchange. "My idea of good company," she reflects, "is the company of clever, well-informed people who have a great deal of conversation; that is what I call good company." Mrs. Smith echoes her words, remarking that "'there is so little real friendship in the world! and unfortunately' (speaking low and tremulously) 'there are so many who forget to think seriously till it is almost too late.'"

Mrs. Smith shows great discretion in keeping her knowledge of Mr. Elliot to herself until assured that Anne has no romantic interest in him. "My heart bled for you," she admitted, adding that "with such a woman as you, it was not absolutely hopeless . . . I was willing to hope that you must fare better." In the end, Mrs. Smith shares the truth about the black-hearted rogue and his role in her financial ruin. "She had previously, in the anticipation of their marriage, been very apprehensive of losing her friend by it." Unlike Austen's mean girls, both Mrs. Smith and Anne Elliot are empaths, thinking before they act.

Sadly, not all of us are so wise.

The media is full of grown-up women harming their peers, whether through competitive motherhood, skirmishes on the career ladder, or petty jealousies over partners. Austen witnessed it as well. Female bullying doesn't get left behind on school grounds; it accompanies us—and Austen's characters—through life.

The sad truth is that people who hurt others have usually been injured themselves. Some act out of fear or even habit; it sometimes feels safer to lash out before another person gets too close. Looking at the big picture, my life is filled with amazing women, both strong and weak. We—I—need to get better at watching one another's back—and never, ever forget Anne Elliot.

Conclusion

Be Kind to Each Other and Read Jane Austen

I do not want people to be very agreeable,
as it saves me the trouble of liking them a great deal.
—JANE AUSTEN

Across the internet, memes declare "Jane Austen is my spirit animal," and "I'm an Austen addict." Facebook pages ask "What would Jane do?" or speculate how "Drunk Austen" would react to today's issues. Clearly, twenty-first-century Austen devotees don't share the Victorian image of Austen as a demure spinster with little agency and an extremely limited worldview. Instead, countless modern Janeites closely identify with Austen's fictional characters, recognizing in them the personal and professional situations we continue to face. Undeterred by the passage of time, Austen readers report knowing—or even being—her characters in their everyday lives.

Five years ago, when I began telling people that I was researching aggression in Jane Austen's work, I met with quizzical expressions. Phyllis Chesler puts it plainly: "Once, feminists needed to believe in 'us', since no one else did. For a while, such faith was heroic, the stuff of which sanity is fashioned." Yet, "to now insist that all women are sisters, or that most women including feminists are kind, or even polite to each other, or that such niceties rise to the level of morality or justice is foolish and self-destructive."

For some reason, even highly educated people think Austen novels are full of placid women in beautiful bonnets. Despite being a literary trope for millennia, female relational aggression slips under the radar—its subtle nature has only received social scientific attention since the 1990s. Understandably, it goes against much of what we have been conditioned to believe. Girls are meant to be "sugar and spice and everything nice"; mothers are the "angel in the house."

Like so much hostility between women, Jane Austen hid her observations in plain sight. She may not have depicted dueling damsels, but her heroines certainly faced enough societal frustrations to make anyone angry and ready to lash out. Except for Fanny Price, each of her protagonists genteelly bares her teeth at some point in her narrative.[1]

Female relational aggression may not seem a pressing social issue either in our own or in Austen's era. Nevertheless, it's in these small things that our world and Austen's coexist on what she referred to as her "little bit (two inches wide) of ivory on which I work with so fine a brush."

It's easy to romanticize Austen's world. Film adaptations offer us lovely dresses, panoramic views of the Peak District and Bath's Royal Crescent; time slows to sips of tea and social calls. Nevertheless, women's lives were—and remain—precarious. We've all heard the reports on how the pandemic affected women more than men. Shouldering the lioness's share of child and eldercare, it has been an incredibly trying time. Despite advances, we continue to confront unique constraints, learning from early childhood to develop competitive strategies that reduce the strength of other girls and how to prevent retaliation.

You'd think that knowledge would change everything, yet as I write this my heart mourns for a friend's fifteen-year-old daughter being bullied by other girls at school. Her crime? She is different in those completely insignificant ways that (usually) only matter to teenagers. She breaks my heart.

---

1. For those who like the ideal of *literally* dueling damsels, simply google "Jane Austen's Fight Club." You're welcome.

If investigating Austen has taught me anything, it is to take concerns like hers seriously. Telling her to "develop a thicker skin," or that "sticks and stones may break my bones, but words will never hurt me" isn't enough. It's a big fat whopper of a lie that is costing lives. As a society, we need to listen.

CONSIDER BIBLIOTHERAPY

Of course, women and girls with clinical depression or suicidal thoughts should seek out mental health professionals. For others, bibliotherapy might be an alternative. The American Library Association (ALA) explains that the notion of using books as a cure for what ails you is nothing new. The ancient Greeks and Egyptians both considered books to be beneficial; King Ramses II even labeled his library "House of Healing for the Soul."

The practice has many names, including biblioguidance, bibliocounseling, literatherapy, and book matching to name just a few. Bibliotherapists use selected reading materials to offer "guidance on the solution of personal problems through directed reading."

Literature—and Austen in particular—has long been known to be a balm in trying times. Austen brought comfort to men in the trenches, camps, and hospitals of World War I. Examining the use of books as therapy during the Great War, Ivy League librarian Theodore Wesley Koch wrote "all we know is that those brave souls find their comfort and consolation in reading, for they tell us so and ask for more." Many offered guidance for the setup of wholesome reading material for the mentally and physically wounded. Koch emphasized that only books helped the men "forget for a few minutes, an hour perhaps."

Modern bibliotherapy isn't so very different. Subjects are paired with a trained bibliotherapist who invites them to explore their relationships with books and examine the types of literature that impacted their lives in the past. During one-on-one sessions, they guide readers to works that help them examine their thoughts and feelings in new ways. For the most part, bibliotherapists prescribe fiction, although some readers respond well to creative nonfiction, poetry, and philosophical texts.

We needn't look far for examples of authors instinctively applying Austen during critical times in their lives—just look at the one in your hands. Others include Rachel Cohen's *Austen Years: A Memoir in Five Novels*, Sophie Andrews's *Be More Jane*, and William Deresiewicz's *A Jane Austen Education*. Bibliomemoir is an emerging genre allowing all of us to peek at other people's bookshelves and the power of the written word.

If nothing else, Jane Austen offers a safe platform to examine our own behavior. There's a reason why book sales rose during the pandemic. Kate Skipper of British book retailer Waterstones explains that "so many people have turned to books for sustenance, information, and joy through this difficult year." We are hungry for stories that distract us from the ongoing COVID-19 slog.

Austen reaches to us from other corners of our bookshelves. Not only are there any number of nonfiction books about her novels, but also scores of authors depict their characters engaging with Austen across genres. It's not mere entertainment. For example, the heroine of Jodi Taylor's sci-fi *Chronicles of St. Mary's* uses the novels for comfort and reassurance. The bestselling YA thriller *Firekeeper's Daughter* shows two matriarchs applying Austen as a common language. The Native American teen narrator explains that "Austen has mediated their tumultuous relationship" throughout her lifetime. Somehow, "spirited discussions about Englishwomen of the early nineteenth century were the only time they could spar on equal footing."

SCIENCE OFFERS INSIGHT

Scholars have been trying to explain the emotional effects of literature for decades, using paper-based reader reflections to identify personal connections to the written and spoken word. Reader-Response theorists suggest Austen remains ageless by triggering shared experiences.

With the emergence of functional MRI technology, neuroscientists can now look within our minds to understand how different types of engagement with texts affect our brains. Stanford University researchers literally used chapters of Austen's novels to determine that reading increases blood flow to different areas of the brain depending on if we are merely skimming a chapter or reading it closely. The results indicate that reading is a valuable type of mental exercise.

Other scholars are investigating how reading activates fundamental units of our brains and nervous systems called mirror neurons. These special types of neurons fire both when we do something as well as when we simply read about it. Linked to empathy, it's why many of us immediately want to scratch our scalps when we read about a case of head lice. It's why we cry out of frustration with Elinor Dashwood and share Catherine Moreland's moonlight panic when her candle goes out.

In *Why Do We Care About Fictional Characters?* literary scholar Blakey Vermeule posits that our connection to Austen is based on our identification with her creations. Vermeule celebrates growing interest in "understanding literary experience not as some ineffable mystery transmitted from on high by a quasi-secular priesthood but as a human phenomenon that can be tested, measured, and defined in ever more precise terms."

I'm up for it if it means more time for reading.

Applying scientific findings to fictional relationships may seem unconventional; past scholarly approaches to Jane Austen's work have rarely included the voices of real readers. Academics tend to look down on Facebook chats about Charlotte Lucas's sexuality or speculating if Mary Bennet ever wed. Nevertheless, looking at the personal experiences of Austen's audience may offer a small window of opportunity for post-pandemic study of the importance of cultural goods. Even before COVID-19, humanities departments across the United States, United Kingdom, and Australia have faced "academic prioritization," often reducing or eliminating arts programs in favor of career-focused disciplines. At the same time higher education is focusing more and more on getting their graduates straight into employment, the nature of work is changing. The pressure to perform has led to increased rates of sickness, absence, and burnout. Pairing literature with STEM subjects may be humanities education's only hope.

If there ever was a time to value the healing qualities of literature, it's now.

STRANGERS ARE EASIER TO HATE

Austen describes female experiences so deeply embedded in human social interactions that it's doubtful that any woman comes to Austen without some sense of recognition. Linking Austen with evolutionary, psychological, anthropological, and sociological findings encourages self-reflection on the reality of women as individuals, each bound by unique hopes and fears. When faced with scarcity, women attempt to protect themselves and their kin both physically and emotionally through female misogyny. It may not be fair, it may have ugly consequences, but it is a reality.

Sadly, there is no simple antidote. If there is competition for scarce resources—however trivial they may seem—there is likely to be conflict. Confronted with female relational aggression, victims may find that identifying the source helps, whether a lack of money, power, agency, time, or affection. Getting to know other women's reality may be the only way to really combat the mean girl phenomenon. Each of us has faced scarcity or insecurity somehow, even super-popular rich girls in cheerleader skirts with their suburban cul-de-sac lives.

Wealthy Caroline Bingley doesn't want to die alone. Isabella Thorpe seeks freedom. Lucy Steele hopes to better her life. Mrs. Norris wants to feel important. This book contains just a fraction of the countless parallels between contemporary psychological phenomena and Austen's descriptions of human behavior.

Speaking with other Janeites, many describe having lifelong relationships with Austen's characters, often reporting that their attitudes toward them evolve over time. In our youth, many lean toward Elizabeth Bennet of *Pride and Prejudice*, a novel that Austen herself worried was "too light, and bright, and sparkling." As we age, we turn to the "shade" and "long periods of sense" in Anne Elliot and begin comprehending the panic in the hearts of Mrs. Bennet and Charlotte Lucas. Our ever-expanding understanding of their realities parallels our growing knowledge of ourselves. Literary essayist Susannah Carson claims that it's common that we find our preferences "shift from one novel to another over time." After all, Carson relates, "the Austen we discover in adolescence is not the same Austen we return to later in life." As we age, our sympathy for her mean girls increases and our blind affection toward her heroines wanes.

Good or bad, these women are no longer strangers.

Of course, Austen depicted positive female relationships as well as toxic ones. Elizabeth adores both her sister Jane and Charlotte Lucas. Elinor is protective of Marianne, despite her tearful drama. Even Fanny Price learns to love Mary Crawford, despite resenting her appeal to Edward. The same is true in real life. "There is plenty of evidence to show that women do indeed support one another," sociologist Marianne Cooper reports. For Cooper, this readiness is linked directly to how highly a woman identifies with her female peers. Women who recognize themselves in others respond to chauvinism with "an increased desire to create more opportunities for other women." Cooper claims that we can encourage more intra-gender solidarity by increasing the number of women around us. "When women work with a higher percentage of women," Cooper posits, "they experience lower levels of gender discrimination and harassment."

In other words, it takes more than a token to make a difference. Only after significant representation is achieved do women experience increased organizational support and decreased gender-based pay gaps.

KARMA ISN'T ALWAYS A BITCH

In fairy tales, Cinderella's stepsisters are punished, Rapunzel's kidnapper dies, and Snow White prevails against her evil stepmother. Austen's meanies don't end as neatly. At most, they are disappointed, left to make snide remarks about the lack of lace at a wedding, or reduced to infrequent visits to Pemberley. Just like us, Elinor will be forced to see her difficult in-laws at the holidays. Elizabeth Bennet will have to hear Lady Catherine's advice on packing until the end of her days.

While reading a Regency novel is not a cure for the ills of society, I—and millions of others like me—find comfort in Austen. She doesn't offer us a blueprint for success. There are no clear winners or patent solutions in her fiction. Nevertheless, there is strength in recognition and solace in Jane Austen.

Useful Resources

If, like me, you were shocked at the numerous reports of young girls committing self-harm after being bullied by peers, here are a few of the many resources available to seek help:

Emergency: 911
National Bullying Prevention Website: www.stopbullying.gov
National Domestic Violence Hotline: 1-800-799-7233
National Suicide Prevention Lifeline: 1-800-273-TALK (8255)
National Hopeline Network: 1-800-SUICIDE (1-800-784-2433)
Lifeline Crisis Chat (online live messaging): https://suicideprevention
   lifeline.org/chat/
Self-Harm Hotline: 1-800-DONT CUT (1-800-366-8288)
Essential local and community services: 211, https://www.211.org/
Planned Parenthood Hotline: 1-800-230-PLAN (7526)
American Association of Poison Control Centers: 1-800-222-1222
National Crisis Line—Anorexia and Bulimia: 1-800-233-4357
GLBT Hotline: 1-888-843-4564
TREVOR Crisis Hotline: 1-866-488-7386
TransLifeline: https://www.translifeline.org 1-877-565-8860
Suicide Prevention Wiki: http://suicideprevention.wikia.com

Rachel Simmons

Educator and author of *Odd Girl Out, Odd Girl Speaks Out, The Curse of the Good Girl: Raising Girls with Courage and Confidence,* and *Enough as She Is,* Rachel shares valuable articles and tips for parents on her website, www.rachelsimmons.com/resources.

Cultures of Dignity

Rosalind Wiseman, author of *Queen Bees and Wannabes: Helping Your Daughter Survive the Cliques, Gossip, Boyfriends, and Other Realities of Adolescence*, created the nonprofit Cultures of Dignity to work with communities to "shift the way we think about young people's physical and emotional wellbeing." Their website, www.culturesofdignity.com, offers a variety of resources for schools.

Better Help

If you can afford it, I highly recommend the service www.BetterHelp .com. Working with a therapist in my own language, from my own state, I got incredibly valuable insight into some of my closest female relationships. The website also hosts numerous free articles, podcasts, and guidelines on subjects like social anxiety and bullying.

Victims of Narcissistic Abuse

If you recognize Lady Susan in your own mother, www.narcissistic abusesupport.com lists support groups and resources for victims in the United States.

Select Bibliography

Benenson, Joyce F. "The Development of Human Female Competition: Allies and Adversaries." *Philosophical Transactions of the Royal Society B.* vol. 368.20130079, 2013, 1–11.

Brown, Donald E. *Human Universals.* 2nd ed. New York: McGraw Hill Professional, 2017.

Carroll, Joseph. *Literary Darwinism: Evolution, Human Nature, and Literature.* Oxford, New York: Routledge, 2004.

Chesler, Phyllis. *Woman's Inhumanity to Woman.* New York: Thunder's Mouth Press/Nation Books, 2001.

Deresiewicz, William. *A Jane Austen Education: How Six Novels Taught Me About Love, Friendship, and the Things That Really Matter.* New York: Penguin Books, 2011.

Flesch, William. *Comeuppance: Costly Signaling, Altruistic Punishment, and Other Biological Components of Fiction.* Cambridge, London: Harvard University Press, 2007.

Gottschall, Jonathan. *Literature, Science, and a New Humanities.* Cognitive Studies in Literature and Performance. New York: Palgrave McMillan, 2008.

———. *The Storytelling Animal: How Stories Make Us Human.* Boston: Mariner Books, 2012.

Johnson, Claudia L. *Jane Austen's Cults and Cultures.* Chicago: University of Chicago Press, 2012.

Keen, Suzanne. *Empathy and the Novel.* Oxford: Oxford University Press, 2007.

Makowski, Sarah. "Jane Austen's Mean Girls: A Biocultural Approach to Shared Female Experience in Literature and Life." Aachen: Dissertation, RWTH Aachen University, 2021.

Richardson, Alan, and Ellen Spolsky. *The Work of Fiction: Cognition, Culture, and Complexity.* Aldershot: Ashgate Publishing Ltd., 2004.

Spacks, Patricia Meyer. *Gossip.* New York: Knopf Doubleday Publishing Group, 2012.

Stone, Lawrence. *The Family, Sex and Marriage in England 1500–1800.* London: Weidenfeld and Nicholson, 1977.

Trivers, Robert. "Parental Investment and Sexual Selection." *Sexual Selection and the Descent of Man*, 1871–1971. ed. B. Campbell. Chicago: Aldine, 1972, 136–79.

Vaillancourt, Tracy. "Do Human Females Use Indirect Aggression as an Intrasexual Competition Strategy?" *Philosophical Transactions of the Royal Society B.* vol. 368.1631, 2013, 1–7.

Vaillancourt, Tracy, and Jaimie Arona Krems. "An Evolutionary Psychological Perspective of Indirect Aggression in Girls and Women." *The Development of Relational Aggression.* ed. Sarah M. Coyne and Jamie M. Ostrov. Oxford: Oxford University Press, 2018, 111–26.

Vaillancourt, Tracy, Jessie L. Miller, and Aanchal Sharma. "Tripping the Prom Queen: Female Intrasexual Competition and Indirect Aggression." *Indirect and Direct Aggression.* ed. Karin Österman. Frankfurt am Main: Peter Lang, 2010, 17–32.

Vermeule, Blakey. *Why Do We Care About Literary Characters?* Baltimore: The Johns Hopkins University Press, 2010.

Weisser, Susan Ostrov. "The Wonderful-Terrible Bitch Figure in Harlequin Novels." *Feminist Nightmares: Women at Odds: Feminism and the Problem of Sisterhood*, ed. Susan Ostrov Weisser and Jennifer Fleischner. New York: New York University Press, 1994, 269–82.

Weisser, Susan Ostrov, and Jennifer Fleischner. "Introduction." *Feminist Nightmares: Women at Odds: Feminism and the Problem of Sisterhood*, ed. Susan Ostrov Weisser and Jennifer Fleischner. New York: New York University Press, 1994.

Wilson, Edward O. *Consilience: The Unity of Knowledge.* New York: Alfred A. Knopf, 1998.

Yaffe, Deborah. *Among the Janeites: A Journey through the World of Jane Austen Fandom.* New York: Houghton Mifflin Harcourt, 2013.

Zunshine, Lisa. "Why Jane Austen Was Different, and Why We May Need Cognitive Science to See It." *Style* 4, no. 3 (2007), 277–99.

———. *Why We Read Fiction: Theory of Mind and the Novel.* Theory and Interpretation of Narrative, 2nd rev. ed. Columbus: Ohio State University Press, 2012.

CPSIA information can be obtained
at www.ICGtesting.com
Printed in the USA
BVHW072252230123
656823BV00003B/3